Kinergetics

Kinergetics

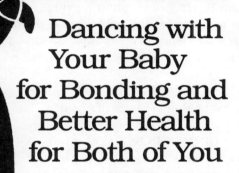

Dancing with
Your Baby
for Bonding and
Better Health
for Both of You

SUE DOHERTY
ILLUSTRATED BY MICHAEL WILSON

BARRICADE BOOKS INC
New York

Published by Barricade Books Inc.
61 Fourth Avenue
New York, NY 10003

Printed in the United States of America.

LIBRARY OF CONGRESS CATALOGING-IN-PUBLICATION DATA
Doherty, Sue.
     Kinergetics: dancing with your baby / Sue Doherty.
        p.   cm.
     ISBN 0-9623032-3-2
        1. Infants (Newborn)—Care—Popular works. 2. Exercise for
women. 3. Mother and infant. 4. Postnatal care. I. Title.
     RJ253.D64 1993
     613.7'1—dc20   93-19657
                                                CIP

First printing, March 1994

Dedicated to Barney, Blake, and Cara

Acknowledgements

Thanks to all the talented singers and musicians that help us express ourselves through dance. My children, although no longer babies, find immense pleasure in dance. To Blake and Cara, thanks for all the magic moments we have and will continue to share.

Many people were extremely helpful as this book emerged from the first drafts. First and foremost is my endearing husband, Barney. His gracious heart, fertile mind, and boundless energy guided me through this challenging course of writing. Thanks for standing by me, Moondoggie.

I am indebted to Denise (Denny) Tibbetts. Her enthusiastic dedication to movement therapy and infant development is invaluable. Years ago my long time friend, Paula Bernhard, introduced me to yoga, for which I will always be thankful.

Heartfelt thanks to Ken Maley, who took the time to counsel a stranger looking for guidance.

While I thought video might be the best medium for this message, he persuaded me to go book first. You were not only right, but warm and generously helpful. At the same time encouragement came from Joy Berry, Dr. Dean Edell, Lon McKuen, and Joannie Greggains.

Ann Mark's companionship, encouragement, and artistic talents are greatly appreciated. What a great logo. In a similar light my deepest thanks and genuine appreciation for dedication beyond the call of duty go to illustrator Michael Wilson. Thanks for being there for me, Michael.

For their kind support and helpful suggestions, I would like to thank Maureen Milla, Gayle Banks, Margie Haggen, Laurie Winkler, Cora Loveland, Susan Williamson, Evan and Katherine Metzger, Megan and Sharon Milan, Brittany and Mac Felton, Rebecca and Mike Healy. The manuscript was a simple glimmer of promise before it benefited from the gifted editorial assistance of Annete Gooch, Susan Watrose, Tammy Parr, and my dear sister, Ann Ross, whose wit and wisdom I cherish.

Sincere gratitude to the following distinguished professionals who took the time and interest to read this work in manuscript. The first one to respond, and the most influential, was Ashley Montagu. It is our great fortune that he was so prolific a writer and humanist extraordinaire. His words shall inspire and guide me throughout my life. I will hold dear his message, "Dance is everything, dance everyday." Thanks go to these very busy and important people that went out of their way to advise and acknowledge my efforts: James G. Garrick, Katherine Kersey, Chris Evert Mills, Bertrand Cramer, and Burton White.

Legal counsel was graciously given by Ed Anderson and Brad Bunnin, my thanks for their guidance and advice.

The people at Barricade Books helped make this work a better read and more accessible to all those ready to dance. Special thanks to Lisa Beck, Vicki Rosenberg, Jon Gilbert. Things as they are, none of this would matter if not for Carole and Lyle Stuart. A resounding thanks for reaching out and allowing me into your quality house of publishing.

Finally, for your support through the years from a wonderful family, Mom and Dad (Deacon Norman and Elsie Ross), Mike and Jim Ross, the Milla family, and Ben and Annabeth Doherty, thank you.

Contents

"If we are indifferent to the art of dancing, we have failed to understand, not merely the supreme manifestation of physical life, but also the supreme symbol of spiritual life . . . For dancing is the loftiest, the most moving, the most beautiful of the arts, because it is no mere translation or abstraction from life; it is life itself."

© by Havelock Ellis. *The Art of Dancing.* Boston: Houghton Mifflin Co. (1923).

Introduction

The magical moments we share with our baby seem unforgettable. The way we wrinkle our noses, the morning sunlight upon our baby's face, or the day's end with a favorite lullaby must last forever. Unfortunately many memories fade or blur. But the warm embraces, graceful movements, and fascinating sounds of music you and your baby enjoy while dancing together will be easily recalled. That is what this book is all about.

Much of our children's attitudes and characteristics will stem from their earliest family experiences and relationships. It is this premise that I will highlight throughout this book. Dr. Bruno Bettelheim, in his most recent work, *A Good Enough Parent*, states that "the importance of early experiences thus rests on the fact that they set the stage for all that comes later, and the earlier the experiences are, the more emphatic their influence."

Dancing with your baby, or what I call "Kinergetics," is a pleasurable activity with shared benefits equally distributed between adult and child alike. Kinergetics influences infants developmentally and offers the caregiver both physical and emotional rewards.

This book combines ideas from psychiatry, bio-mechanics, child development, health and fitness, preventative back care, and music and movement therapy. Research in psychiatry and human development underscore the importance of touch and its role in fostering a child's security. The way our brain develops and the significance of positive human and environmental stimulation in shaping the quality of this emerging landscape is explored.

Music is a key ingredient in shaping a stimulating play environment for parents and children. I will take a closer look at music, its role in other cultures, and how listening to music, and the movement from dancing to it, has therapeutic value for you and your growing baby. How all this specifically relates to the special needs of the exceptional child will also be discussed.

Stress occurs in everyone's life. This common by-product of life is often compounded by the obligation of nurturing a family. Exercise, and Kinergetics in particular, can go far in easing tension. You and your baby's life will prove more manageable, and your stress will be transformed into a zest for life in this first precious year together. I discuss this at length in chapter 7: "The Anti-Stress Factor."

Stretching, sports fitness, weight lifting, and aerobic conditioning are popular today. The latest information on these subjects, as well as proper back care, body mechanics, and safe weight-lifting of your baby are incorporated in this book. You will also find information about the safe carriage of your baby and the correct body alignment for each movement. This approach, while helping you tone your body, will also sharpen your parenting skills.

Now that you have a new baby, you can start to enjoy dancing together immediately. Slow, graceful ballroom style dancing will be soothing to the youngest of infants if held close and securely to your body. Only when your baby has gained sufficient control of its head should you begin to dance more energetically. This comes at approximately three months, when the muscles in the neck become strong enough to support the raising of the head when lying, or to maintain an upright head position while sitting.

Kinergetics is an activity that needs no special apparatus—no expensive exercise equipment and no giant balls or tunnels. Your little one will provide all the weight you need for training and toning your muscles. Your baby will be thrilled to spend the time with you in this playful interaction. Kinergetics is simply a matter of turning on the music and lifting your baby in dance; a mutually gratifying experience.

With every experience and each passing moment babies are influenced developmentally. Such daily occurrences as bathing, feeding, playing, singing, rocking, and changing clothes are all part of an infant's course of learning. Place a rattle next to a baby and it facilitates visual stimulation. If the baby chooses to play with the rattle, then tactile motor stimulation occurs, which can stimulate speaking. The way in which the baby reacts attracts our attention and motivates a response from us verbally and with a smile.

Adults communicate with babies in many different ways—looking, talking, holding, rocking, singing, smiling, touching, laughing, and listening. Kinergetics offers fascinating interaction in all these ways for your youngster, along with a vigorous workout for you. This unique approach is soothing and stimulating for you and your baby.

To properly and safely execute these movements with your baby, I suggest that you first read this book thoroughly. Then, study the illustrations and read the accompanying instructions. Finally, reread the instructions as you slowly go through the movements.

As you introduce your infant into your home, I would like to welcome you to your new world as a first-time parent, or make greater your existing world as an experienced family. This is a book for you and your baby, and for all caregivers of young children. May the bonds be formed with loving strength and so endure the future years.

"For a parent's love to be fully and positively effective it ought to be enlightened by thoughtfulness. Everything we do, as well as how and why we are doing it, will make a conscious or more often unconscious impact on our child."

Kinergetics: What's It All About?

Welcome to Kinergetics. An activity shared between baby and mother, father, or caregiver, Kinergetics is a program designed to enhance child development and provide a low-impact aerobic workout to music while dancing with your infant. To pick up your baby and dance may be a natural tendency for some parents and caregivers. In this book I take the impulse one step further by introducing you, the primary weight-bearer, to various ways of carrying your child that will increase your aerobic exercise, improve your awareness of proper back care, and, in the process, introduce you to an activity filled with music and high-spirited fun for the two of you.

If babies could talk, they would tell you quite emphatically: there is something very special about dancing. Surrounded by exhilarating embraces and wondrous sounds of music, infants giggle and respond with excited pleasure to the interaction involved in Kinergetics. Within these pages is a universe of delight for your baby and a world of fun for you as well. You and your child will be partners in this invigorating exchange.

Kinergetics is a term I derived from the words: "kinetic," to move, of or resulting from motion; "energy," to be active or at work; and "energetic," having or showing energy. It is also taken from the word "kin," meaning kindred, relatives, family, or kinsfolk.

The idea for Kinergetics was born after my first baby and I visited an infant stimulation class taught by my good friend Denise Tibbetts. I remember how anxious I was to see what Denny was teaching. I felt a bit isolated living in a remote corner of the California wine country. I also knew what a dedicated movement therapist Denny was and what enthusiasm she brought to her work with children of all ages. Although it was almost a two-hour trip to the Head Over Heels Gymnastics Center in Oakland, it was time to learn something new about parenting. I was also eager to show off how much my little boy, Blake, had grown in the four months since his birth. It would be especially entertaining for Denny, who happened to be at Blake's birth, to see how he had changed.

The room was filled with moms and babies, and many brightly-colored play things. There were hammocks to sway them in, tunnels for them to crawl through, large balls to place your infant atop, and chin-up bars suspended from the ceiling encouraging their grasp. We had fun discovering them all, but what made the most lasting impression was Denny's helpful introduction to a couple of different ways to hold your baby and dance to the accompanying music, which created a movement therapy session for the babies.

Back home I elaborated on this new information, incorporating my favorite exercises, stretches, and dance steps. I danced almost daily with Blake and later with my second child, Cara, and always found it tremendously fun for all of us. It proved to be won- derful exercise for me, and fulfilled the need to enter- tain my infants who demanded nearly constant interaction and insisted on being held much of the time.

The goal with Kinergetics is to provide benefits for the two of you: for the adult, to exercise and reduce stress, and perhaps lose excess pounds from a recent pregnancy; for your child, to create a stimu- lating environment, intensify bonding, and improve language and sensorimotor development. Infants whose senses and muscles are stimulated become more receptive to their surroundings than babies who do not receive such stimulation. Learning takes place as infants absorb and organize the information they see, hear, taste, smell, and feel, by physically moving about, and through social play. The National Association for the Education of Young Children's manual for caregivers entitled, *Developmentally Appropriate Practice*, edited by Sue Bredekamp, warns us not to neglect to provide a sensorimotor enriching environment. "If infants are deprived of many opportunities to sample a variety of sensory and motor experiences, their emotional and cognitive development will be hampered." Kinergetics is a high-quality, age-appropriate play experience.

This upbeat, often spontaneous interaction will brighten your day and help create a healthy environment in which your infant can thrive. When Kinergetics becomes a familiar activity the routine will give your baby a sense of security. In time your attentiveness will aid your infant in learning that it has control over his* environment. Bonding or attachment develops from answering your baby's cries quickly and consistently, and from adult cues that tell your baby he is worthy. Bonding also develops with dancing, cuddling, touching, and repeating eye to eye glances of joy. This has a beneficial effect on a baby's ability to feel confident in the world. The chance to interact happily with adults in

---

*To avoid the exclusive use of male pronouns, I will use "he" for the child in the first half of the book and "she" in the second.

a variety of ways is the single most important kind of play for your infant. Through it your baby learns that other people are responsive, and fun to be with.

A MONTH BY MONTH LOOK AT
DANCING WITH YOUR BABY

All babies need comforting. The actions that are most accepted and thus effective are those that recreate life in the womb. The smooth, gentle, rhythmical motion and touch of dance is dramatically reminiscent of life as a fetus. Babies are remarkably sensitive to the special quality and familiar appeal of dance. Babies thrive under such affable care. The carriages or holds that I will be referring to are illustrated and discussed in chapter 12: "Dance Steps and Carriages For Baby."

The First Month: Newborns have a range of sight from eight to ten inches. This is where you should be when face to face dancing. Carriages that allow for close eye-to-eye contact will be the best during the first month. Baby's muscle and nervous systems are immature at this age, as is their sense of balance. Physical development for newborns will be reflexive. Muscular control will be seen with the grasp reflex, startle reflex, and the tonic neck reflex. Only the

"Over the Heart Embrace" and the "Rock-a-bye Cradle Hold" are appropriate at this age.

Physical discomfort of mom, and post-partum blues, creates added stress. For many of you, your needs will blend with baby's here, as you both benefit from gradual, graceful, slow and easy moves. All the floor exercises (for moms only), especially sit ups, are very helpful during these first few weeks after delivery. For illustrations and instructions refer to chapter 13: "Stretching It All Out."

The Second Month: Life with your baby is becoming more routine now, you know better what to expect, and you become more confident in your parenting skills. Your baby's eye-to-eye contact, which began in the first weeks, is progressing to more of a prolonged gaze. You may begin to observe his imitation of your facial gestures; the first social smile may emerge. The start of a reciprocal relationship has begun, your baby's ability to interact socially is budding. At this very young stage, an infant becomes sensitive to your emotions as demonstrated by your pleasurable expressions, and he is able to connect that to his own happiness. Your mutual sensitivity to each other's happiness is the foundation upon which strong attachment to one another develops. When the first smile day arrives, it seems to bring with it an increased desire by caretakers of infants for playful exchanges—a wish to go beyond caring for the routine physical needs like bathing, feeding, and changing clothes and diapers. Keep up the gentle dance moves and recommended carriages for infants too young to have head control. (See the first month.)

Between the first and fourth months the muscular control of your baby's head and neck will progress from simple turning to holding the head upright without support.

The Third and Fourth Months: Between the second and fifth month infants are still unaware that they are, in fact, separate from their mothers; they feel more like their mothers are an extension of themselves. Usually an established eating, sleeping, and playing schedule has occurred by this time. A parent now realizes that they are quite capable of knowing what their baby needs. This understanding, and positive interpretation of the baby's signals, are carried over during dance time. Together their mutual sensitivity has matured, intensifying the relationship with increasingly greater contentedness.

By this time the playful dance may intensify as your baby's physical strength matures. More and more carriages and dance steps are possible and welcomed with open arms. You are now able to incorporate more stimulating carriages and moves like "Fly Like a Bird," if you carefully support your baby's neck and chin area. At approximately four months of age infants commonly show head control. When this occurs, most of the other carriages may be incorporated into your dance together, with the exception of the "Fireman's Carry." The floor exercises, where the adult supports the infant in some manner, may also be included now.

The Fifth Month: By the fifth month your baby will have initiated more autonomy. A sense of security will develop. This becomes more noticeable as you witness the increased willingness of your infant to be left to his own world of self-discovery after the dance with you is over.

Between approximately four to eight months of age the infant's physical development with muscular control progresses from the ability to hold his head up independently and in midline position, to holding his head up when on back, stomach, and sitting. Sometime during this age infants will sit unsupported for a short time, are able to lean back and forth, and may push themselves to a sitting position.

From here on all carriages are appropriate for any infant showing muscular strength in the neck and head area. The floor exercises, which rely on the adult to support baby in some way, are also appropriate.

The Sixth and Seventh Months: Boredom buster. Kinergetics can give you relief from what after six months may have become mundane. Lift up your spirits with a little dance. Energize yourself and watch your baby really encounter his autonomy enthusiastically after your dance together. You've satisfied him and he's amused. He's stronger, sitting up, rolling over, and maybe crawling. If baby is sitting up by himself, all carriages and floor exercises may be used.

The Eighth and Ninth Months: From approximately eight to twelve months of age the infant's muscular control of the trunk and legs has matured to allow him the ability to raise himself to a sitting position, sit alone, stand with some support from furniture or people, stand without assistance, sit from a standing position, and finally, to squat and stand.

Stranger anxiety puts you front and center, on top of the number one most loved list. His relationship with you magnifies to such a point that he trusts only you. When in your arms, though, he's more daring than ever. Now's the time to try the "Fireman's Shoulder Carry." The "Fly Like a Bird" carry can be as energetic as you both please—soar like an eagle, fly like a dove.

The Tenth to Twelfth Months: Your baby is becoming more and more mobile—some may be walking already, or well on their way. Enjoy the whole Kinergetics routine. As the primary weight bearer of this little bundle of joy, your muscles will be getting a real workout now. Many babies are easily twenty or more pounds.

RESOURCES

BOOKS

A Good Enough Parent, by Bruno Bettelheim (New York: Knopf, 1987).

To Listen To A Child, by T. Berry Brazelton (Boston, MA: Addison-Wesley, 1984).

The Art of Sensitive Parenting, by Katherine Kersey (Washington, DC: Acropolis Books, 1983).

The First Six Months, by Penelope Leach (New York: Knopf, 1987).

The Human Connection, by Ashley Montagu (New York: Columbia University Press, 1979).

Parent Power! A Common-Sense Approach to Parenting in the 90's and Beyond, by John Roseman (Kansas City, MO: Andrews and McMeel, 1990).

MAGAZINES

Parents, 685 Third Avenue, New York, NY 10017

American Baby, 10 East 52nd St., New York, NY 10022

Parenting, 301 Howard St. 17th Floor, San Francisco, CA 94105

Child, P.O. Box 3173, Harlan, IA 51593-2364

Healthy Kids: Birth–3, 475 Park Avenue South, New York, NY 10016

Mothering, P.O. Box 1690, Santa Fe, NM 87504

Working Mother, 230 Park Avenue, New York, NY 10169

ORGANIZATIONS

American Academy of Pediatrics (AAP)
141 Northwest Point Boulevard
P.O. Box 927
Elk Grove Village, IL 60009-0927
708-228-5005

Black Child Development Institute
1028 Connecticut Avenue, NW
Washington, DC 20036
202-387-1281

Children's Defense Fund
122 C Street, NW
Washington, DC 20001
202-628-8787

Infant Development Education Association (IDEA)
c/o Catherine H. Thompson, RN, MSN
Department of Education
Mary Washington Hospital
Fredericksburg, VA 22401
703-371-2712

Foundation for Child Development
345 East 46th Street.
New York, NY 10017
212-697-3150

"While you are showing your baby things and calling his attention to more and more interesting experiences in his world, you are also drawing his attention to the most interesting things of all: yourselves."

CHAPTER 2

The Personal Connection: Touch

Loving touch is at the heart of parenting. Showing intimacy through warm embraces will elicit dramatic responses from your baby. As you approach, your baby will reach forward, wiggling and giggling with delight. But after demonstrating his excitement to see you, your baby will watch for your reaction, hoping he has been successful in mobilizing you to act. When you do respond he will follow with a burst of new energy. It is through this rewarding and animated exchange that your baby learns what it is to be a social human being.

Of all our senses touch is the most important. Without sight and hearing we are able to survive. Our sense of taste may leave us without significant consequence, and our sense of smell rarely seems operable once we fall asleep. But without an ability to respond to touch, we are socially and emotionally lost, barely surviving, with little comfort and mental health.

Our impulse for physical contact is intense at birth. We immediately derive information and sensations through the skin, the body's largest organ. The warmth from bodily contact and the sensation of a beating heart are essential to life. When we are comfortably in the hands of a loved one it sends vital impressions that help our brains to develop and function. Touch generates the production of chemicals which the brain relies on to feed our blood, tissue, nerves, organs, and hormones. So dependent is our body on feeling, that the lack of touch sensations would starve us.

We are able to see, hear, taste, and smell by ourselves, but it is our sense of touch that most often requires another's presence. In fact, touch has a power unlike our other senses, it can give great pleasure to others. Tickle a baby's foot and see the delight it brings and hear the laughter it produces. A tender stroke of a hand upon his little head can often sooth the most overwhelming troubles. It's the magic of a loving caress from one who cares that brings pleasure and a satisfying attachment between people. Touch has the capacity to communicate kinship and well being. Walt Whitman said it best when he wrote in "Song of Myself": "I make holy whatever I touch or am touch'd from."

For roughly 6,000 hours fetuses tumble head over heels in a warm caressing liquid. The womb is a small world full of touch, with the rhythmic heart-beat amplified audibly and physically, blood rushing through the umbilical cord, and the rocking and swaying of mother's steps. This touch and move-ment, so vital to life in the womb, should continue after birth.

The University of Virginia Medical School studied the effects of touch on nearly one hundred children. Early stimulation, such as rocking and close physical contact, contributed significantly toward reaching developmental milestones such as memory, language, sight-spacial problem solving, and comprehension of new information. With the need for human touch and interaction satisfied, the recipient feels deeply loved, which nurtures the ability and desire to learn and perform.

Babies must, however, experience a certain amount of autonomy. The ability to discover the joys and frustrations of the world and to rely on oneself to draw out information from the surroundings is of supreme importance. It is in this way that an infant develops an understanding and love of his own self. These influential times of separating and self-exploring come easier to a baby after its basic phys-ical and playful interacting needs have been met. You will find that Kinergetics fulfills these concerns in such a delightful manner that your little one will be quite content to explore on his own.

Kinergetics gives you an opportunity to express affection in a unique way for your baby through physical contact. Dancing with your baby establishes a firm basis of trust and support, developing the desire and confidence to pursue physical activity. In the end it fosters language development and self-expression in your child. Babies listen to the sounds around them. Music and singing can encourage an infant to be vocal. If you take this opportunity to repeat the sounds they make it will coax them to imitate sounds. By doing so your baby will begin to gain control of language and learn the process of mutual communication. This participation leads to a fuller life for your baby emotionally and intellectually, and helps strengthen the bonding process. A baby who is thriving and happy also provides an atmosphere with reduced stress and tension. In all these ways, Kinergetics provides a foundation for a most positive family relationship.

What young babies require most is loving attention, not toys. Through Kinergetics, you are fulfilling, in a most delightful way, your infant's most vital needs, to be held, loved, touched, and enjoyed.

RESOURCES

BOOKS

The Earliest Relationship, by T. Berry Brazelton and Bertrand G. Cramer (Reading, MA: Addison-Wesley, 1990).

Touching: The Human Significance of the Skin, by Ashley Montagu (New York: Columbia University Press, 1971).

The Aware Baby: A New Approach to Parenting, by Aletha Jauch Solter (Goleta, CA: Shining Star Press, 1984).

The First Relationship, by Daniel Stern (Cambridge, MA: Harvard University Press, 1977).

A Parent's Guide to the First Three Years, by Burton White (Englewood, NJ: Prentice-Hall, 1980).

The Therapeutic Touch, by Dolores Krieger (Englewood, NJ: Prentice-Hall, 1979).

ORGANIZATIONS

La Leche League
9616 Minneapolis Avenue
Box 1209
Franklin Park, IL 60131-8209
708-455-7730 (800-La Leche)

Association of Maternal and Child Health Programs
2001 L Street NW, Ste. 308
Washington, DC 20036
202-775-0436

"The shaman's song of power, and the ecstatic, trance-inducing dance demonstrate the true power of rhythm and sound. They are gateways to a dimension with which our civilization has lost touch. One thing is certain: Song and dance are no mere symbols, but an expression of an inner psychophysical attitude that leads to a change in consciousness and brings us nearer to the pulse of life and thus to ourselves."

Dreamtime and Inner Space: The World of the Shaman by Holger Kalweit. © 1984 by Holger Kalweit and Scherz Verlag, Bern and Munich (for Otto Wilhelm Barth Verlag). Translation © 1988 by Shambhala Publications, Inc. Reprinted by arrangement with Shambhala Publications, Inc., 300 Massachusetts Ave., Boston, MA 02115.

CHAPTER 3

You As Movement Therapist

When you dance with your baby you are practicing a form of healing. Movement therapy teaches that dance is a powerful force that can bring changes to a participant's inner and outer realities. As a partner in the dance the caregiver will benefit in many ways. Kinergetics is therapeutic for the adult, but it has far greater social and emotional advantages for the child.

While dancing, we help infants to see, hear, and feel themselves and their immediate surroundings. As our favorite music fills the air, our baby twirls around with us and feels the support of our strong arms lifting him. Holding your baby face-to-face for an eyeful exchange, and then turning him outwards to view the beauty of the day through a picture window, enlivens our baby's senses. By playing in this way babies create a self-identity.

Our physical and emotional involvement contributes to our children's sense of individuality and self-worth. The infant begins life actively kicking and flailing arms involuntarily. This is followed by intentional actions of thumb sucking and hand play, and voluntary movements of the legs and arms. All the while he receives and reacts to body needs fulfilled. All of this leads to an awareness sometime within the first months that his body is physically distinct. Sandra Anselmo, in *Early Childhood Development*, explains how social cognition develops from the way an infant perceives other people. When adults repeatedly respond to signals of discomfort, babies learn they are separate by experiencing a unique voice, touch, and odor. As Anselmo puts it, "Infants gradually gain a sense that they are effective individuals who can exert partial control over their experiences by summoning adult relief. This sense of effectiveness is a critical early cornerstone of self-concept." Kinergetics opens up an array of psychophysical therapeutic experiences. To augment the holding of a baby with the enjoyable motion of dance, to add the melodic variety of music to the sounds of street or home, and to create visual stimulation by frequently changing their perspective enriches their lives.

Kalweit writes, "It has been said that the person who has rhythm has the world." Because of the internal rhythms within our bodies, such as respiration, heartbeat, and other organ functions, and the outside world of tides, seasons, and planetary movements, there seems to be a universal interconnectedness. Some believe that our internal kinetic flow of energy is an extension of the natural movement of the earth and universe. When we become aware of our inner sense of rhythm and our perpetual need for movement, we experience a feeling of inner harmony. Music assists us in outwardly expressing these feelings. Manfred Clynes, a neuroscientist and a renowned leader in the study of emotional responses to music, succinctly states: "Music moves. Not only emotionally, but bodily: music dances inwardly and incites to gesture, to dance, outwardly." In the words of music therapist Barbara J. Crowe, "Music, then, becomes the voice of the great cosmic oneness." This belief provides you and your baby yet another means of connecting with each other.

There are some infants whose need for this type of stimulation is greater, perhaps because of a lack of other adequate stimuli. The benefit of dance is great for exceptional children adjusting to illness or impairments, or children who experience any oppressive environment. The expressive caring and multiple stimulation that Kinergetics brings might ease these early difficult times. All infants become overwhelmed with their new world periodically and will become distressed. You may alleviate these disturbing feelings by dancing with your baby, which sends them a strong, positive, non-verbal message.

In many cultures neutralizing emotional conflict is the duty of a shaman (a priest or medicine man in some religions of the world). The shaman uses ceremonial enactments to vent the fears and emotional conflicts of a community or individual. There are distinct similarities between music and movement therapists and the shamans found in every region of the world.

The shaman's rituals are often filled with music and dance. Our Kinergetic activity is similar to that of a shaman's. The priest's religious rites maintain social balance and control in harmony with the elements of nature. With Kinergetics we seek to restore social balance by instilling composure, contentedness, and the natural feeling of belonging. The primary caregiver of an infant is, for the child, an empowered guide. He or she is a magical leader, offering safety and comfort from an unknown world in a natural atmosphere of trust and belief. Our role as our child's shaman is to fulfill their needs by immersing them with us in a caring and rhythmic embrace. The part we play is necessary since infants continually search for integration with their new world.

In many cultures, a shaman uses a drum to summon feelings. The drum becomes the driving force of expression. The adult participant, upon hearing the drum beat, starts to dance. It is this movement, together with the sounds they hear, that entices the child's expressive interaction. Babies are consistently discovering their bodies' ability to move. Because of such exploring they progress from new-borns with reflexive movements to babies gaining muscular control.

The dance process does not have to be dependent on the use of music. If music seems to bring pleasure to an infant, it adds another stimulus to their surroundings. But the movement, the visual stimulation, and the closeness to you, will provide an adequate healing atmosphere, even without music. The lack of sound should not stop you from dancing with your baby. There may be times when an infant will find more comfort in gracefully moving about with you, in a peaceful quiet setting.

Kinergetics is the ultimate pacifier. It always seemed amazing to me how satisfied my children were after I had danced with them. As young babies they would often fall asleep in my arms while I was slowly dancing. Delighted with the experience, they also were happy sitting, lying, or exploring on their own. This led to long periods for me to do whatever I wished. That quiet time was a wonderful reward for something I enjoyed just as much as they did.

RESOURCES

BOOKS

Dreamtime and Inner Space: The World of the Shaman, by Holger Kalweit (Boston, MA: Shambhala Publications, Inc., 1988).

Movement and Drama in Therapy, by Audrey Wethered (Boston, MA: Plays, Inc., 1975).

Dance and Movement Therapy—A Healing Art, by Fran J. Levy (Reston, VA: The American Alliance for Health, Physical Education, Recreation and Dance, 1988).

ORGANIZATIONS

American Dance Therapy Association
904 Walnut Avenue
Baltimore, MD 21229

Institute for Expressive Analysis
c/o Dr. Arthur Robbins
325 West End Avenue, 12B
New York, NY 10023

The American Alliance for Health, Physical Education, Recreation, and Dance
1900 Association Drive
Reston, VA 22091

"After birth, appropriate auditory stimulation promotes emotional, social, and language development. Soothing, pleasant, and interesting sounds inspire curiosity and a receptive attitude toward language. A variety of sounds are important, one at a time. Music, voices, and even household noises such as refrigerators or dishwashers are good raw material, but a constant background of music or machinery noise makes sound discrimination difficult for babies. A noisy and confusing environment can be detrimental to development."

© by Dr. Jane M. Healy. *Your Child's Growing Mind* (page 31). New York: Doubleday (1987).

CHAPTER 4

The Sounds of Music

Music is a catalyst that awakens motor response in you and your child. When the beat goes on, you have to move. The growth of your baby's intelligence depends on a sensorimotor process, the child's response to the environment through the use of senses and muscles present at birth. Thinking and learning through the senses become established in infancy. Musical sound is more than a magical world for your baby, it may heighten his development more than we realize.

While in the womb, the first rhythm a baby hears is its mother's heartbeat. In utero infants coordinate their pulse and breathing to match their mother's. Once born, the breast with a beating heart beneath it reminiscently offers the newborn comfort. Even the most passive babies become energized with rhythmic sounds. U.C.L.A. Medical Center's Infant Stimulation Education Association research indicates that premature infants who have "listened to" the classical music of Brahms, Bach, and Beethoven gained weight faster than those without such auditory exposure.

Music can divert attention away from discomfort. When listening to music, complex brain chemistry changes occur in the brain stem which controls heartbeat, respiration, and muscle tension. The physiological effects include an increase in blood volume, stabilization of heart rate, and lowering of blood pressure. Some doctors and musical therapists support the theory that natural painkilling chemicals in the brain known as endorphins are released as a result of exposure to music. These natural opiates secreted by the hypothalamus reduce the intensity of pain. Strong musical beats can be calming by influencing you to breathe deeply and rhythmically. Music can relax you and your baby. Few would dispute that relaxation is universally therapeutic.

Robert Brody, writing in the April 1984 issue of *Omni* magazine reported on a study conducted at the Dusznikachzdroju Medical Center in Poland. The study involved 408 patients suffering from headaches and painful neurological diseases. It was shown that listening to music for therapeutic purposes significantly lowered the need for medication for some patients when compared with a control group.

Music therapy has also shown benefits for insomniacs, mental patients, and women during the process of childbirth. These studies demonstrate the potential benefits of listening to music for both parent and child. Dr. Frank Wilson, a neurologist and author with a particular interest in auditory perception feels strongly that music can foster self-esteem. He argues that exposing our children to music will advance their social, emotional, and language development.

Early Western philosophers believed that music could influence a person's thoughts, emotions, and bodily health. The Greek philosopher and mathematician, Pythagoras, prescribed a daily routine which included listening to music upon awakening, working, relaxing, and falling asleep. Another Greek philosopher, Aristotle, wrote:

". . . emotions of any kind are produced by melody and rhythm; therefore by music a man becomes accustomed to feeling the right emotions; music has thus power to form character, and the various kinds of music based on the various modes, may be distinguished by their effects on character—one, for example, working in the direction of melancholy, one encouraging abandonment, another self-control, another enthusiasm, and so on through the series."

Today the importance of music is often over-looked in our stress-filled world. Unlike our prede-cessors, we often neglect to recognize music as a powerful art capable of immense influence on society and individuals. We witness a staggering variety of musical sound and are able to hear recordings of music everywhere we go: in offices, grocery stores, and even elevators. Music is often used as a passive force, a sort of background noise. Kinergetics favors the conscious selection of music to enhance our well being, as well as our children's.

For the adult participant in Kinergetics, music increases the ability to perform movements with grace and rhythm. Selecting music that appeals to you is the most important consideration, although you will want to avoid music that is overstimulating to your baby or is excessively loud. Your baby will cue you in if, to him, the music you select is disrup-tive or annoying. Watch for signs of discomfort: he may cry, fidget, or stiffen his body. Your mood and your musical taste for pop, jazz, Motown, country, classical, new age, light rock, rhythm and blues, or anything else, will most likely change from one day to the next. Feel free to experiment.

Irish jigs and Scottish reels always bring forth a joyful spirit. Dancing to them makes for a lively, good-humored experience. Similarly, such ethnic music as African drumming, Caribbean rhythms, and Greek, Arabic, and Japanese folk music, offer many possibilities to explore various dance steps. America's own musical heritage: fiddle tunes, early ragtime, or much of contemporary country music, is wonderful to move about to and pleasing to hear for all ages. The rich vocals of country artists such as Garth Brooks, Vince Gil, Kathy Mattea, Dolly Parton and many others add nicely to the toe tappin' beat.

Older siblings may have records or tapes that are fun to dance to as well. Dancing to juvenile music selections such as lively renditions of old familiar folk songs and nursery rhymes spark the older children to participate. It is lovely to see them join in, swirling and skipping about with a cuddly doll or stuffed animal. Dig through their musical collection and put on Raffie, "Wee Sing," or Paul, Tom and Annie of Backwood Jazz. To include other family members or caretaking youngsters will help create a home environment that makes everyone feel good.

To get you moving the range of musical possibilities are bountiful. Explore a variety of musical styles. You may wish to experiment with classical marches, or perhaps, Mozart's *Don Giovanni*, Mendelssohn's *A Midsummer Night's Dream*, or Arthur Fiedler's *Anthology of Marches* played by the Boston Pops. Use these powerful pieces with discretion and play them softly. You can also dance gracefully and with vitality to dances and songs from Broadway shows or movie soundtracks. An array of suitable choices exists that can trigger your desire to get up and dance. Let your musical imagination free in making selections.

Hal Lingerman states in *The Healing Energies of Music* that listening to beautiful music has the ability to heal, inspire, attune, and expand spiritual consciousness. He suggests that if you are emotionally tense to listen to such works as Debussy's "Claire de Lune" or the Adagio (3rd Movement) of Rachmaninoff's Second Symphony. He also says that quiet music will often serve to quell angry feelings by acting to rebalance you, often moving you toward constructive activity. Recommended listening for this purpose includes Bach's Two Concertos of Two Pianos, Handel's Harp Concertos, Halpern's "Ancient Echoes," and Roth's "You Are The Ocean." To relax and instill loving feelings try Vivaldi's Oboe Concertos, *Parkening Plays Bach* (guitar solos), Mahalia Jackson's *Miscellaneous Hymns*, and J.S. Bach's *Jesus Joy of Man's Desiring*.

Additional music that will be soothing to the youngest of infants includes Gregorian chant music, Brahms' Lullaby, J.S. Bach's Two Flute Concertos, Mozart's Piano Concerto No. 21, Pachelbel's Canon in D, and Tchaikovsky's Waltzes from *Sleeping Beauty, Swan Lake,* and *The Nutcracker.* These last selections are of particular importance to newborns, premature or special needs infants, and the hyper-sensitive baby who needs quiet sounds to comfort him.

Gregorian chants likewise provide exceptional children the experience of hearing all the frequencies of the voice spectrum and a most peacefully energizing sound that soothes and comforts. The rhythm is one of a tranquil heartbeat. A chant has no meter, the human breath accounts for its timing and often increasingly long phrases arise from the chants. The art of singing a chant is dependent on controlled exhalation that has the physiological effect of slowing down the rate of breathing and so slows down the heartbeat. Those engaged in listening to Gregorian chants may find their breath similarly slowed down and blood pressure and heartbeat reduced.

The following is a list of some of my favorite music for Kinergetics.

For slow warm-up or cool-down:

The Music of Turlough O'Carolan played by Duck Baker et al. (Irish Harp music from the 1700's played on guitar and flute)

John Coltrane Quartet—*Ballads*, with McCoy Tyner on Piano

Vivaldi—Mandolin Concerti, German String Orchestra, Behrend conducting

Nanci Griffith—*Little Love Affairs*

Van Morrison—*Hymns to the Silence*

Dolly Parton, Emmy Lou Harris,
and Linda Ronstadt—*Trio* album

Go For Baroque with pieces by Handel, Bach,
Pachelbel, and Vivaldi

Van Cliburn—*The World's Favorite Piano Mix*

Gregorian chant music

For the more active portion of the dance (If some
selections on albums are too intensely electrictified
subjecting an infant to overly loud stimuli, be sensitive and skip to the next selection):

Paul Simon—*Graceland*

Bonnie Raitt—*Nick of Time*

Dire Straits—*On Every Street*

Van Morrison with The Chieftains—*Irish Heartbeat*

The Chieftains—*An Irish Evening* with Roger Daltrey
and Nanci Griffith

David Grisman Quartet—*Acousticity*

Steve Goodman—*Say It In Private*

Kathy Mattea—*A Collection of Hits*

Norman Blake (with Doc Watson and Tony Rice)

Big Chill soundtrack

Itzhak Perlman—*Ragtime Music of Scott Joplin*

James Taylor—*Never Die Young*

Antonio Carlos Jobim—*Classics*

Darol Anger and Barbara Higbie—*Live at Montreaux*

What a joy hearing music is for children. We never grow too old to enjoy listening to music. It is a wonderful way to introduce new sounds to your baby. Many infants start to sing along; you may also. When you witness the level of enthusiasm with which your baby greets you as you turn on familiar music (or even music that is not so familiar) and dance together, your self-esteem will flourish, along with your baby's.

RESOURCES

BOOKS

Music—Physician for Times to Come (An Anthology), by Don Campbell (Wheaton, IL: Quest Books, 1991).

The Healing Energies of Music, by Hal A. Lingerman (Wheaton, IL: Quest Books, 1983).

The Secret Power of Music, by David Time (New York: Destiny Books, 1984).

Live Music Therapy, by Peter Nunez Cardoza (Burnet, TX: Live Music Therapy Press, 1988).

ORGANIZATIONS

American Association for Music Therapy
355 Crossfield
King of Prussia, PA 19406
215-265-4006

National Association for Music Therapy
8455 Colesville Rd., Ste. 930
Silver Spring, MD 20910

"Infants get information through their senses and motor activity. When infants interact with their environment, they are doing something. Infants use all their senses. With experience they refine their capacities for seeing, hearing, smelling, tasting, and touching. Moving themselves, moving others, and handling objects become coordinated with their senses."

CHAPTER 5

The Thinking Side of Babies

The second trimester of pregnancy marks the onset of a rapid development of brain cells (neurons) which continue to develop for twelve months. Following this initial formation of neurons, glial cells form, acting like glue to hold them together. An interconnecting pathway emerges, sending messages from cell to cell and linking them with each other, providing an efficient relay network. This system of cells provides the necessary materials for intelligence throughout life. These neurons must be arranged in a systematic fashion to allow for thinking, perception, and recalling information.

The landscape now emerging, which allows for thinking, does not occur automatically. The quality of this developing system is partly dependent on environmental stimulation. Neurons send messages back and forth building new connections as sight, sound, and touching stimuli are received. Each neuron has hairlike receptors known as dendrites, the growth of which is responsive to environmental influences. Cells which are activated to transmit information develop new dendrites branching into a tree-like form. This dendrite action is one of the main factors in the growth of the weight of the brain during childhood. Jane Healy, education psychologist and author of *Your Child's Growing Mind*, says of this phenomenon, "Amazingly, although the number of cells remains almost the same, brain weight can double during the first year of life." According to Dr. William Sears, author of *Growing Together—A Parent's Guide to Baby's First Year*, researchers have demonstrated that nerve cells change size depending on the environmental input. In experimental animals, the weight of the brain increased in an atmosphere rich with stimuli.

When a child becomes interested and involved in his surroundings, synapses and neural systems form. With each successive exposure and response to varying stimuli the connections become more distinctive. The capacity of the brain to think or respond increases as demands are placed upon it. By creating a stimulating environment, Kinergetics activates this wonder of human life.

Learning begins with visual-spatial activities that require touching and feeling people or objects and by acquiring a feeling of one's own body in space. Child development researchers now believe that stimulation as a result of rocking is essential to the development of the cerebellum and the vestibular system. Located at the top of the spinal cord, the cerebellum contains structures for reflexes and basic motor coordination. The vestibular system is the control center for balance. Dancing, like rocking, provides infants with comfortable experiences of movement, which excites the cerebellum and vestibular system.

As a fetus, the infant experiences a rocking motion as the mother moves in addition to the self-initiated swimming-like movements in the uterus. Many authorities agree that this rocking continues to be vital to developmental advancement and healthy emotional growth after birth. In general, touch by frequent holding, rocking, swinging, and other physical stimulation is important to an infant's robust growth.

Dr. Ashley Montagu, a renowned social biologist, maintained that an infant requires an additional nine months after birth where he experiences a "womb-like" environment to incite brain development. Adults who hold their young close to their bodies in snug back or front carriers while shopping, walking outside, or going about household chores, are recreating this womb-like environment. Kinergetics is a perfect example of this recommended style of carrying an infant.

The first months in a child's life provide a framework in which he rehearses bodily gestures toward a variety of environmental stimuli. During this sensorimotor stage, until about eighteen months, the brain is not equipped to handle anything beyond immediate physical experience.

Today's infant development researchers view babies as characteristically curious, socially involved, and surprisingly mature in their cognitive abilities and emotional reactions. It is now understood that babies engage in play to further their wellbeing. They seek to draw information in and decipher it. They have the capacity to distinguish complicated vocal rhythms and to exhibit specific preferences for particular tastes and sounds. Even while only a few months old babies are recalling information learned and starting to imitate the actions of others who are dominant in their lives. Some studies have shown infants less than four days old who copied the behavior of people who stuck out their tongues at them, and some imitated emotional expressions of happiness and sadness. (Appendix I offers an approximate timetable for developmental milestones reached by the first fifteen months of life.)

A young child's self-image is formed in part by the discovery of how his body moves. Before he can speak or understand his thoughts, his body is his basic tool for dealing with his world. An infant develops from head to toe and from trunk to arms and legs, slowly learning to control his body and realizing that they are all part of him. With this knowledge he discovers the space, sounds, and textures of his immediate environment. By participating in dance together we can support this awareness thus promoting the growth of a healthy personality.

Language development also responds to this type of concerned, involved approach to parenting. With responsive caregiving a child recognizes that his cries or calls for attention are answered. Reactions such as this motivate your baby to cultivate emerging language skills, and also encourage your baby to become more and more sociable. Sensitivity to our children's cares serves to increase all the collective processes of the growing infant.

All infants are individuals with unique characteristics in temperament, in activity level, and in their response to various stimuli, such as sound, light, and touch. A primary caregiver must be sensitive to an infant's individual needs, becoming intimate with their behavior patterns, and tailor their parenting accordingly.

For hyperactive or overly sensitive infants the environment preferred may be a dark room with no sounds, or low, soft music and a calming, secure, and gentle embrace from a parent. Above all, being aware of a baby's particular needs will avoid compromising his healthy development. These hyperactive children are often difficult and test a parent's patience. Responding appropriately to their specific needs may lessen any hardships and aid in the child's overall development.

For the infant who prefers not to be too confined by a close embrace, dancing with them may be just the right move. Some babies are so engrossed with observing their surroundings that they feel their view of the world is too narrow when held closely over your heart; what they are rejecting is merely "how" they are being held, not being held per se. These infants may enjoy being carried facing outwards while dancing or walking. Try varying how you hold your baby until you find the most comfortable position.

A child's behavior engages both body and mind reaction. Babies react to varying stimuli in differing ways. As the distinguished pediatrician T. Berry Brazelton explains, some infants will overreact to any single sound or stimulus by crying, throwing up, becoming frightened, or having a bowel movement. Other babies will respond in a more internal fashion, showing little outward emotion. They may lie alert and peaceful, and be very conservative with their physical response, which allows them close observation of the stimulus. Although these are opposite responses, both reactions are normal. As these children grow older they may cope with stress in a similar manner as they did in infancy, one crying persistently and the other finding comfort from sleep.

Taking into account individual differences while doing Kinergetics is essential to its principal goals. Focus closely on the ambiance of the room, the way in which you dance, the quality and volume of the music, and the carriage your baby prefers from one moment to the next—for all of these will influence your baby's response to the combined stimuli. Kinergetics does not have to be an overwhelming experience for overly sensitive infants if you temper your dance and music to their particular likes. It may help smooth the way toward a more relaxed infant who feels that he can cope better now with your help.

If you and your baby feel good about Kinergetics then keep doing it. If it is not working out well at first, it may in a month or two. Be open to reevaluation and change. Whenever you choose to engage in Kinergetics, there will come a time, during each dance, when your baby has reached his limit. Younger infants often fall asleep in your arms while you slowly dance; still others may begin to wiggle and squirm indicating they've had enough. (For my older children it was I who tired first.) Watch for this and be receptive. Your baby will learn that quiet time by himself often follows this period of intense physical interaction. The time period following Kinergetics will strengthen your baby's sense of autonomy.

Kinergetics relies completely on a feedback system in which the adult participant must be attentive to the infant's signals. It is an intimate exchange that shows caring and concern, and communicates love.

RESOURCES

BOOKS

Your Child's Growing Mind, by Jane Healy (New York: Doubleday, 1987).

The Infant Mind, by Richard M. Restak (New York: Doubleday, 1986).

Child Potential: Fulfilling Your Child's Intellectual, Emotional, and Creative Promise, by Theodore I. Rubin (New York: Continuum, 1990).

ORGANIZATIONS

National Association for the Education
of Young Children (NAEYC)
1834 Connecticut Ave., NW
Washington, DC 20009-5786
202-232-8777

Association for Childhood Education
International (ACEI)
11501 Georgia Avenue, Suite 312
Wheaton, MD 20902
301-942-2443

"Put simply, the infant brain, particularly the compromised brain, requires the support of loving parents, good nutrition, stimulation, and love. If ignored or understimulated that brain will never be able to compensate for the subtle functional disturbances that we now know result from low birth weight, prematurity, or combinations thereof.

Care and affection make a difference. Instruction, patience, and stimulation make a difference. Fortunately, the infant brain is incredibly malleable and adaptive; it will make up for what it has been deprived of if given half a chance. There is no room for fatalism or pessimism here. The most important factor of all? Overcoming the disappointment of that mother and that father, consumer-minded, who feel that somehow nature has cheated them by giving them a 'defective product.' If those parents can be convinced of the nearly infinite restorative powers of the infant brain, that child will have a fighting chance."

CHAPTER 6

Special Needs: The Exceptional Child

High risk infants, premature and postmature infants, and babies suffering from congenital or hereditary problems often have impaired interactions with their parents or caregivers. These babies spend so much time and energy battling with their disease, impairment, or premature size that their developmental clock is turned back. Difficulties develop due to the strain from unresponsiveness, colicky or fussy demands, or unsuccessful feeding habits. This often causes caregivers to feel guilty, frustrated, and depressed which in turn hampers positive parent/infant interaction. It is important to remember that a baby who is slower in development is on the same track as the others; his train is moving slower but is headed for the same destination.

A premature infant is naturally weaker and less developed and is less apt to be able to hold his head up to make frequent eye contact. Your baby's attention span may be at a deficit level as well. Such infants often need more stimulation before a response is seen. A lively parent ready to dance may be just right for baby. Great care must be taken to insure that his entire head, neck, and body are well supported at all times.

Premature infants have responded favorably to massage as well, and Kinergetics can be viewed as similar to massage in motion. The motion of dance and your warm caress will physically stimulate your baby's body in much the same way as a massage. But parents must stay alert to their preemie's signals to know when the infant has reached his stimulus threshold.

A family has to be interested in how a child copes with his special needs before significant progress toward improving himself and overcoming obstacles takes place. *The American Baby Guide to Parenting,* edited by Dr. David A. Link, states that, "As parents, you are in the best position to observe your children's development. You can tell if your child is not seeing or hearing properly much earlier than anyone else, and your comments and anxieties should always be taken seriously." You need to discuss your observations and concerns openly with your child's doctor, as well as understand your specific responsibilities.

Such responsibilities may include coping with deafness, feeding likes and patterns, physical mobility limitations, or the unique way special needs children see or don't see their world. Understanding exactly the nature of the condition, the means of care and treatment, the cause and implications of the handicap, and the financial aspects, is vital to competent care.

As a parent, you may feel alone and isolated when you learn of your child's special needs. But early intervention soon after diagnosis helps you and your child develop a positive attitude. It takes a tremendous amount of courage and strength to see past the tragedy of the moment. For the exceptional infant Kinergetics can provide an atmosphere so rich with caring, warmth, and gentle sounds that he will soon understand that in his world all is well. Nurturing this formative relationship is as important as any effort towards elevating the infant's physical condition.

A special needs child will find it terribly difficult to move beyond accepting to adjusting to his condition without the dedicated involvement and encouragement from his family. Environmental maturity starts in the home.

As an infant develops from the sitting stage to crawling, explorations of his surroundings intensify. Propelled to discover the physical world around him he interacts through touching and exploring his findings. With the exceptional baby often this is not possible and his new discoveries must wait for a helping hand. Bringing the stimulus to him, dancing over toward a mirror, lifting him to eye level, holding him outward to view the world, exposing him to the sounds and movements of Kinergetics will be beneficial to him. Early intervention with developmentally appropriate activities can give these children a real head start in adjusting to themselves.

SPECIFIC RECOMMENDATIONS
FOR INFANTS WITH SPECIAL NEEDS

In many infants with handicaps a full intellectual development is a substantial substitute for stunted physical development. It is recognized more and more that not only is emotional development significantly dependent on the early years, but intellectual growth also begins at this time. A special needs infant must become involved in a wide variety of experiences that excite the tactile, kinesthetic, and special senses. Quite early in life the mental processes that accumulate, sort, and store these impressions occur, and will afterward affect more complicated mental work. The initial discovery of a hand quickly evolves to the realization that the hand can reach out and grasp toys of pleasure. It won't be long before blocks are balanced and then toppled, creating new wonders of the imagination. These essential phases, if missed, will obstruct growth in future stages, or frustrate and confuse the child unable to integrate the information sufficiently.

Many pediatric and developmental enhancement programs exist, offering the parent guidance and answers that are important additions to daily care. Some studies conclude that the major impact of early intervention is on the parent's morale, since periodic contact with a specialist in children with developmental disabilities gives parents an ongoing relationship with someone who has a real interest in their child. This contact also strengthens the parent/child relationship by instilling parental confidence and encouragement. Parents who incorporate age and disability-appropriate play at home will dramatically increase the positive benefits already begun by the specialist. A parent is a kind of naturalist, leading the child like a newcomer along an unfamiliar trail, acquainting him with the glory of nature and any pitfalls to avoid on his next traverse.

Moreover, parents receive assistance in recognizing the infant's readiness to progress forward developmentally, and technical information that increases the infant's potential to act on this readiness. The direction taken is one of prevention of any secondary disabilities. Early guided stimulation for the baby opens up his world and speeds up his learning and accomplishments. I urge all parents to make contact with a pediatrician who specializes in children with developmental disabilities for the support and confidence it provides.

Instructions and illustrations for recommended carriages or stretching positions can be found in chapters 12 and 13.

Preterm Babies and Milestones

As a parent of a preterm baby you must relax your expectations about developmental milestones. Questions and anxieties arise during the first year about your baby's progress toward "normal" developmental achievements which have no set answer. There is no definite pattern for premature infants. It's important that you keep in mind the way doctors routinely evaluate a preemie. Until your baby is two or three years of age, you calculate his age according to his due date, rather than his actual birth date.

All babies, whether full term or preterm, vary widely as to when they achieve readiness for another level of development. Preemies in particular may have experienced complications that further slow the process down. They are not behind, due to circumstances — they are right where they should be. Have patience and a watchful eye that looks for your child's signals, and respond to his cues.

Because of their immature nervous system, during the first year some premature infants may be cranky. Additionally, many preemie infants show a tendency to be hypersensitive. Some may have difficulty becoming attracted to stimuli, some may withdraw, feeling that they have encountered too much. This may be the effect of a prolonged hospital stay. The time spent in the intensive care unit is filled with bright lights and noises of the hospital. A low stimulus threshold develops, and times of alertness are short and infrequent. Separation from you may make him cautious and temperamental as well. As your child matures, much of these characteristics will subside, and the infant will become more responsive. Don't mislead yourself into thinking these changes are permanent, for they are temporary. Your baby needs to be seen for the unique individual he is, ready to emerge with a distinct personality all his own.

When you first bring your preemie baby home it may be necessary to temper your urge to stimulate him and get his attention. Don't ignore all forms of stimulus however. Try milder, gentler ways to excite his senses. Slow, melodic, soothing music, natural or dim lights, and graceful, secure embraces over the left shoulder may be quite acceptable to baby. At three or four months of age past due date, his time awake and his attention span will lengthen. He will be ready to actively partake in discovering the world around him.

Doctor Janine Jason, mother of a premature baby and author of *Parenting Your Premature Baby*, remarks, "Touching, rocking, and fondling your baby are all extremely important activities that should not be forgotten . . . Most important, talk and sing to your baby." You can easily heed this advice by dancing with your baby, which incorporates all these suggestions.

During Kinergetics you must carefully support his head, until roughly two months after he passes his due date. However, it is a good idea to strengthen his neck and shoulder muscles by placing him on his stomach, where he will briefly try to hold his head up. During dances you may want to try, for a brief time, the "Fly Like a Bird Hold," which mimics this recommendation. Also, the "Outward Facing Chair Carriage" will be useful in this regard. As baby gradually gets stronger all the carriages and floor exercises will be suitable for baby to enjoy.

Infant Colic

Colic is a condition of several somewhat minor but painful occurrences that can go wrong in a baby's digestive system in the first months of life. Accompanying this symptom is a screaming-like cry which goes on and on, for the baby is unable to be consoled. Efforts to ease the discomfort are only partially effective, giving relief periodically and inconsistently. Physical signs of pain are seen as the colicky infant makes a tight fist, brings up its legs, and pushes its chest forward by arching its back.

It is estimated by some researchers that colic afflicts more than twenty-five percent of the infant population. This behavior is first seen in the five to ten day old newborn. Often the signs of distress begin in the late afternoon and evening. The majority of cases seem to suggest that colicky behavior subsides after a maximum of ten weeks. If the case is a particularly stubborn one it may persist for up to sixteen weeks.

If colic first occurs after the second month, it most likely indicates food allergies or a milk intolerance. It is a simple matter to eliminate milk products from your infant's diet as well as your own, for there is evidence that what mother consumes affects the make up of her breast milk. Eliminating foods one-by-one is the best way to recognize the source of your baby's intolerance.

Some researchers believe that the cause of colic is an obstruction to the passage of gas in the large intestine by local spasm or cramping. To minimize this happening, feed a colicky infant in an upright position, patiently, and carefully burp it, and massage the abdomen gently. It may be helpful to lessen the amount of each feeding and increase how often they are fed. If enough time has passed since the feeding, some gentle dancing may bring relief to an infant's upset colon.

Christopher Farran, a medical writer and author of, *Infant Colic—What It Is and What You Can Do About It*, remarked, "The things that often tend to soothe colicky infants—sucking, swaddling, rocking, monotonous noise or vibration—may 'work' because they interrupt certain nerve impulses or stimuli traveling from the infant's belly to its brain." He goes on to report that many studies have indicated a possible cause of colic is "central nervous system immaturity." Irregular nerve signals controlling the function of the intestines may be smoothed out by motion, warmth, and noise. Kinergetics may be the ideal activity.

Carrying baby in the "Fly Like a Bird Hold" while slowly swaying from side to side and massaging and patting baby's tummy, after a gentle period of an "Over the Heart Carriage," may relieve the infant's pain. Also the "Outward Facing Chair Carriage" keeps your baby in the suggested upright position, which will facilitate the passage of gas in the stomach and intestines. Other helpful moves are floor exercises. For example, lie on your back with legs outstretched. Then bring the knees to your chest and place the baby belly down on your lower legs.

Listening to music that is pleasing to the baby will help to distract him from his discomfort, and will bring relief to him and you.

Infantile Spasms—A Special Form of Epilepsy

Spasms observed during infancy are often mistaken for colic. Epilepsy in infants is easily recognized clinically. The usual signs of a spasm are a sudden flexing of the head or body at the waist, arms rising in a surprised reaction, knees going upward, and short duration crying. Infantile spasms last only a second or two. The baby then relaxes, and shortly thereafter the spasm recurs in the same manner. These spasms occur in a series of five to fifty repetitions before stopping. Many of these episodes may occur throughout the day.

Two essential characteristics between infantile spasms and colic must be distinguished. Colic will not be seen as a series of episodes; and infantile spasms is the only kind of epilepsy where seizures happen in a series.

It is uncommon that infantile spasms would begin before two months of age; generally most start between four and eight months. The good news is that even untreated, this type of epilepsy will slowly fade away during the second to the fourth year of life. How Kinergetics would affect these infants is not clear, so please consult your infant's doctor before engaging in this activity.

Down Syndrome

No parent really anticipates giving birth to a special needs child. Until it happens to you, the odds are simply statistics that happen to others. Down syndrome afflicts one out of every 800 to 1,100 births. It is a result of a chromosome abnormality. Children with this disorder all suffer from mental retardation, however the degree of retardation usually ranges from mild to moderate. Although there are minor distinguishing characteristics in facial features, there are more similarities with other babies than there are differences.

More complicated problems may arise in some children with this syndrome, such as congenital heart defects and hearing loss. More than seventy-five percent of infants born with Down syndrome have some degree of hearing loss.

Dr. Siegfried M. Pueschel, Professor of Pediatrics at Brown University and Director of the Child Development Center at Rhode Island Hospital, wrote a very useful book entitled, *A Parent's Guide to Down Syndrome—Toward a Brighter Future*. In it he says, "At a very early age, the infant responds most to being touched. Touch is a valuable source of information for the infant. Visual and auditory stimulation should preferably be combined with tactile experiences. Probably the most important early sensory experiences for the infant are those of being handled . . . Children usually respond more actively when movements are accompanied by talking or singing to rhythmic tunes. Starting in infancy, several stimuli can be used simultaneously, for example, dancing and singing to catchy rhythms and rhymes while holding the child in differing positions." Kinergetics is "just what the doctor ordered."

Children with Down syndrome process information slowly. It may take more time before you see signs of curiosity. However, with sufficient help from birth onward, learning will take place, and will be continuous. Language development will be as slow as motor skills. These children, with developmental delays, need more time to process a communication. It is certainly important for you to communicate and exchange facial expressions, vocal sounds, and body language with them, but allow the child adequate time to process the information. Silence is okay, wait for a response and don't fill in the void by speaking. But once the child gestures in some way, answer back.

Because of delay in initiating motor skills, the infant with Down syndrome requires outside help to engage in activities. Results from your efforts won't be obvious right away. However, do not underestimate the value of involving your child in regular training of their basic skills. These children can not afford to miss out on important developmentally helpful tools just because results are not readily seen.

You may discover that the very young infant with Down syndrome lies in an uncommon position. The legs often spread apart and roll outward with the knees bent. This atypical position should not be allowed to become a habit or later difficulties in movement may arise when the infant sits or walks. To minimize this tendency, while holding, carrying, or dancing with the baby, bring his legs together until they touch.

The degree of muscle weakness in different body locations varies with the individual. Most often, the young baby with Down syndrome needs greater support of the head and trunk than does the normal infant. Keep their physical limitations in mind whenever you are carrying him about, be it in your arms or in a cloth carrier of some sort. Although the muscle weakness decreases as he gets older, it is important to encourage strong head control as early as possible. Dr. Pueschel recommends only minimal support to the head area, just enough to prevent wobbling about. This will speed up the strengthening of the necessary muscles which control this head-lag position. Therefore, while the infant is in the sitting position, dancing in your arms, or other positions, do not allow your baby's back to always rest against your body.

Kinergetic carriages most suitable for Down syndrome babies include the "Over the Heart Embrace," using your forearm to support baby's back while the hand of the same arm reaches up to support baby's head and neck. The other arm is placed under the buttocks. The "Outward Facing Chair Carriage" is also useful, if enough care is taken to support the head and neck in a similar manner. Reach around with your forearm up the front of the baby's torso and place your hand gently under baby's chin for support. Place the other arm under baby's bottom.

The "Fly Like a Bird Hold" can also be modified for the baby with Down syndrome. With baby face down, wrap one arm around the baby's hips and rest your hand on his tummy, and nestle his legs and body close to you. At the same time take your other forearm and hand to create a gentle resting place for baby's chin and neck area. The "Rock-a-bye Cradle Hold" too offers baby a secure embrace that looks up to caring eyes.

As special babies become older, more challenging positions must be added to facilitate good balance. When baby's position changes frequently, from tilted forward, backward, or sideward, his sense of balance is tested for a reaction. Dr. Pueschel reminds us, "Improvement in balance can only occur if the child makes a strong, active attempt at balancing." With advancing age more demanding Kinergetic carriages may be useful in developing balance reactions. Lift and lower your baby, whether in the above mentioned carriages, or when incorporating the more complex carriages as the "Waist High, Two Handed Outward Facing Hold"; "Resting On Chest, Outward Facing Hold"; "Face to Face, Two Handed Hold"; "Pony Ride Hold"; and "One Arm, Front Facing Outward Carry."

The floor exercises, illustrated in a forthcoming chapter, will be useful in serving the same purpose. Again, with these positions, rock baby forward and back, or side to side, and watch for excessive toppling of the head, but don't give too much support to head and trunk.

RESOURCES

BOOKS

And A Time to Dance, by Norma Canner (Boston, MA: Plays, Inc., 1968).

The Chronically Ill Child and His Family, by Mathew Debuskey, ed., (Springfield, IL: Charles C. Thomas, 1970).

Infant Colic—What It Is and What You Can Do About It, by Christopher Farran (New York: Charles Scribner's Sons, 1983).

Understanding Birth Defects, by Karen Gravelle (New York: Franklin Watts, 1990).

Parenting Your Premature Baby, by Janine Jason and Antonia Van Der Meer (New York: Henry Holt and Co., 1989).

Parenting Children With Disabilities, by Peggy Muller Miezio (New York: M. Dekker, 1983).

A Parent's Guide to Down Syndrome—Toward a Brighter Future, by Siegfried M. Pueschel (Baltimore, MD: Paul H. Brookes Pub. Co., 1990).

The Well Baby Book, by Mike Samuels and Nancy Samuels (New York: Summit Books, 1990).

Your Premature Baby, by Prank P. Manginello and Theresa Foy DiGeronimo (New York: John Wiley and Sons, Inc., 1991).

MAGAZINES

Pediatrics for Parents, The Newsletter for Caring Parents, Pediatrics for Parents, Inc., P.O. Box 1069, Bangor, ME 04402-1069

ORGANIZATIONS

The March of Dimes
1275 Mamaroneck Ave.
White Plains, NY 10605
914-428-7100

American Medical Association
Committee on Rehabilitation
535 N. Dearborn St.
Chicago, IL 60610
312-464-5000

The United Cerebral Palsy Foundation
66 East 34th Street
New York, NY 10016

National Association for the Visually Handicapped
22 West 21st Street
New York, NY 10010

National Association of the Deaf
814 Thayer Avenue
Silver Spring, MD 20910
301-587-1788

National Easter Seal Society
2023 West Ogden Avenue
Chicago, IL 60612

Parent Care (puts out annual directory: *Parents of Prematures Resource Directory* and publishes *Guiding Our Infant Through Preterm Development*)
9041 Colgage St.
Indianapolis, IN 46268-1210
317-872-9913

Parents Helping Parents—A Family Resource Center for Children With Special Needs
(Divisions: Handicaps—Understanding and Group Support; Intensive Care Nursery Parents; Parents of Down Syndrome)
535 Race Street, Ste. 140
San Jose, CA 95126
408-288-5010

Parents of Premature and High Risk Infants International, Inc.
33 W. 42nd Street
New York, NY 10036

National Association for Down Syndrome
628 Ashland
Chicago, IL 60305

Parents of Down Syndrome Children
c/o Montgomery Co. Association for Retarded Citizens
11600 Nebel Street
Rockville, MD 20852
301-984-5792

American Digestive Disease Society
7720 Wisconsin Avenue
Bethesda, MD 20814

The Epilepsy Foundation of America
1-800-EFA-1000

Institute of Physical Medicine and Rehabilitation
New York University
Bellevue Medical Center
400 East 34th Street
New York, NY 10016
212-263-6028

"The adult and infant who can achieve synchrony of signal and response begin to add another dimension to their dialogue. They begin to anticipate each other's responses in long sequences. Having learned each other's requirements, they can set up a rhythm as though with a set of rules."

CHAPTER 7

The Anti-Stress
Factor

While parenting and caregiving are rewarding, they clearly take a heavy toll on the human body and psyche. The physical and emotional stress of being a parent or caregiver, whether full-time or not, is real. At times the responsibility can feel overwhelming and leave us with few emotional resources to tap into in order to cope with the day-to-day pressure. Much of this however, can be alleviated with a sound fitness program. Giving adequate attention to your own physical and emotional well-being will pay dividends in the form of a less stressed-out you and a happier baby. With its emphasis on music and dance, Kinergetics can help reduce much of the stress resulting from physical and emotional fatigue.

Incorporating yoga, stretching, and Tai Chi into your life can be especially helpful in dealing with emotional burn-out. Some people refer to Tai Chi as "meditation in motion," and yoga has a centuries-old reputation for helping to reduce fatigue and soothe

the nerves. Kinergetics offers an introduction to these helpful, anti-stress disciplines.

The absence of the extended family often makes raising children a trying experience. In today's society, unlike your parents and their families before them, where people generally lived close to their relatives, you have the added stress of nurturing much of the time alone. Without the guidance and diversion that grandparents, aunts, uncles, and cousins can provide, you may feel that you have little support as a parent. Worse yet, if you are a single parent, the difficulties of parenting are dramatically compounded. If you feel isolated and stressed from lack of help, you may want to find allied groups and resources. You can enhance your knowledge and understanding of life's processes if you seek out the vast array of valuable information that is available through books, agencies, magazines, professionals, and support groups. For a list of such resources please refer to the appendix and bibliography in the back of this book.

If you are feeling sad, irritable, frustrated, inadequate, etc., and you are keeping these negative feelings to yourself, you are putting yourself under undue stress. By blocking such emotions you inhibit other more positive emotions from surfacing. Tell your baby or older child or children how you are feeling, open up to your husband, wife, mother, father, doctor, minister, or therapist. And express your positive feelings too, verbally and with actions like dancing with your baby. Older children love to dance too—any which way. The dance and open communication will help you find that relief, even if briefly, from the demands of parenting.

If you are a parent home all day, you may feel frustrated that you give so much to your baby and yet it doesn't ever seem to satisfy him. Babies' needs flood in as persistently as the high tide and their happy times come and go like the ebb and flow of the sea. Parents working outside the home have the added burdens of finding and keeping competent care, dealing with pangs of guilt and frustration from lack of time with their child or children, and feelings of actually being relieved to be away from their demands.

Depression can also be an element of stress and may occur because of post-partum hormonal shifts. It may also develop when certain expectations are not met. Hurt and rejection arise when the baby, or anyone else, does not meet our expectations. Thoughts focused more on you and not on the needs of others can trigger anxiety. Finding the joy in serving and meeting the needs of others can erase some of the difficulties we may encounter in our lives. Just being active will help, be it exercise, happily meeting the needs of others, or seeking the help of others for yourself.

The exercise from Kinergetics will help relieve stress, but it won't hurt to get even more exercise. Again I would urge you to include your baby. That can easily be done with walking. An excellent form of exercise, brisk walking can be shared with your baby as he rides along in a front pack or back carrier. If possible, when your baby is napping, arrange for a sitter and, go for a run, bike ride, or tennis game. Being on your own, doing something for yourself will refresh you when you return to your child.

Your stress and the stress your baby feels from times of separation will be relieved or tempered a great deal by time devoted to close, uninterrupted, long-lasting one-on-one physical and emotional contact. The benefits are greatest if time for closeness occurs before and after times of separation. If you are a working mother, it will prove to be a relief from feeling divided between career and home pursuits.

For further reading on this subject, I highly recommend *Holding Time* by Martha G. Welsh, M.D., a Fireside Book first published in 1989 by Simon and Schuster Inc. Dr. Welsh's underlying principles of "holding time" directly parallel those of Kinergetics.

Dr. Welsh's method of parenting is becoming acknowledged and practiced in Europe and the United States. I feel it is essential reading as a means to continue the bond between you and your baby and to fortify or reestablish the attachment between you and your older child or children.

Dr. Welsh relies on the theory that the neurobiology of attachment produces two chemicals in the brain. The hormone noradrenaline, acts to arouse the brain in such a way as to cause a decline in clinging behavior. Endogenous opiods are released when a child is stimulated by a caring caress from his mother and are believed to decrease anxiety due to separation. Her belief is that infants and toddlers activate these two systems by going back and forth between autonomous play and close contact with their mother, thus regulating strong emotions. Balance of these two brain chemicals of arousal is unlikely if a child does not get the needed response from his mother. This inability to adequately fulfill his need for exploration and physical contact will cause hyperactivity in the child. It is this premise that Dr. Welsh underscores as the basic necessity for what she calls, "holding time."

If your baby is colicky, hyperactive, or irritable for any reason, or if you are fatigued, better than escaping for a much needed break away from their demands, try getting closer. Going off to the movies, dinner, or shopping will only aggravate feelings of unhappiness and frustration. Dr. Welsh suggests staying in bed together until you and your baby both start to feel relief. Take the time to rest.

I never allowed myself to feel guilty for wasting time by lying in bed with my child, usually on top of me. I would try to sneak away after I felt rested, requiring much less sleep than my baby did. To be honest, my youngest, Cara, who is four, still enjoys lying down on top of me as I rest on the couch from time to time. This, despite the fact that she isn't a daily napper. Again, I slip away after my rejuvenating twenty minute cat-nap has done its job. I love these times. It is recommended that for the more disturbed children to stay in close contact until resolution of the stress occurs. Being there when he wakes up may be necessary. And when you feel trapped by the clutches of a clinging toddler or pre-schooler whose jealousy is obvious and demands are nerve-wracking, when going to the bathroom seems like torture for them, you might seriously consider not only quality play time but sincere holding time.

You are most likely familiar with and able to identify unpleasant feelings you have, but how do you decifer your child's feelings, beyond their crying? A few of the signs of insecure attachment, according to Dr. Welsh, include: crying or fussing excessively, refusing to make eye contact, some eating and sleeping disturbances, reacting strongly to small changes in their routine, an inability to mold to your body while being held, an immediate attempt to be put down as soon as they are picked up, and being overly content for long periods of time in their crib or playpen.

Holding Time will be of great value for any family where tantrums or sibling rivalry are problems. It is a difficult adjustment for a youngster to accept sharing his mother even if he is getting a brother or sister. That is not how he sees it. In his eyes he is only losing, unless you demonstratively show him otherwise.

P.S. A SHORT NOTE ON CHILD ABUSE

There is a consensus among experts on child abuse and neglect that a variety of causes contribute to make parents susceptible to becoming abusive. These include the way a child behaves, the lack of social support in raising the child, and the stress resulting from financial concerns or marital problems. Being the primary caregiver to a young child is extremely demanding and at times even overwhelming. There is no doubt it affords a magnitude of stress difficult to withstand. Our mind often becomes so weary that we are unable to deal effectively with certain situations.

The dangers of this kind of stress gone awry can lead to child abuse. If you find yourself close to losing control, you can try what some doctors and music therapists recommend: listen to music. If your attitude becomes calmer, pick up your baby and dance together.

Child abuse often begins with an adult having a history of being abused themselves as children. Whether it is through neglect, or sexual, physical, or emotional abuse, authorities say more than thirty percent of those mistreated pass on such hurt to the next generation. We need to stop this vicious cycle of pain. Not only will we have better adjusted children and adults, but we will see one major cause of aggressive behavior and drug and alcohol abuse eliminated.

If you lose control of your ability to handle a stressful situation and have an urge to inflict harm or verbally abuse your baby, you may need professional help. If you feel you need help, or know of someone who does, please seek assistance from one of the many support groups and agencies listed below.

R E S O U R C E S

BOOKS

Mother's First Year: A Coping Guide for Recent and Prospective Mothers, by Cynthia Copeland Lewis (Whitehall, VA: Betterways Pub., 1989).

Growing Young, by Ashley Montagu (Boston, MA: Bergin and Garvey, 1989).

The Self-Calmed Baby, by William A. H. Sammons (Boston, MA: Little Brown, 1989).

Growing Together: A Parent's Guide to Baby's First Year, by William Sears (Franklin Park, IL: La Leche League International, 1987).

The Relaxed Body Book, by Daniel Golman (New York: Doubleday, 1986).

Whole Body Healing: Natural Healing with Movement, Exercise . . . by Carl Lowe (Emmaus, PA: Rodale Press, 1983).

MAGAZINES

The Single Parent, Parents Without Partners, Inc., 8807 Colesville Rd., Silver Spring, MD 20910

Today's Family, 27 Empire Dr., St. Paul, MN 55103

Twins, The Magazine for Parents of Multiples, P.O. Box 12045, Overland Park, KS 66212

Working Mother Magazine, Lang Communications, 230 Park Ave., New York, NY 10169

Self, 3500 Madison Avenue, New York, NY 10017

Psychology Today, 24 E. 23rd Street, New York, NY 10010

ORGANIZATIONS

American Association for Marriage and Family Therapy
1100 17th St., NW, 10th Floor
Washington, DC 20036
202-452-0109

COPE (Coping with the Overall Pregnancy/Parenting Experience)
530 Tremont Street
Boston, MA 02116
617-357-5588

Family Service Association of America
44 East 23rd Street
New York, NY 10010

Bureau of Community Health Services
Office of Maternal and Child Health
Public Health Service
U.S. Department of Health and Human Services
5600 Fishers Lane
Rockville, MD 20857

Head Start Bureau
Office of Human Development Services
Administration for Children, Youth and Families
U.S. Department of Health and Human Services
Washington, DC 20201

Single Parent Resource Center
141 W. 28th Street, Ste. 302
New York, NY 10001
212-947-0221

Women On Their Own (Parents)
P.O. Box 1026
Willinboro, NJ 08046
609-871-1499

Family Therapy Network
7705 13th Street, NW
Washington, DC 20036
202-829-2452

National Committee for the Prevention
of Child Abuse
332 South Michigan Avenue, Suite 1250
Chicago, IL 60604-4357
312-663-3520

The American Humane Association
Children's Division
63 Inverness Drive East
Englewood, CO 80220
303-792-9900

C. Henry Kempe National Center for the Prevention
and Treatment of Child Abuse and Neglect
1205 Oneida Dr.
Denver, CO 80220
303-321-3963

Parents Anonymous
6733 South Sepulveda Blvd., Ste. 270
Los Angeles, CA 90045
In California: 213-388-6685
Outside of California: 800-421-0353

Parents Without Partners
P.O. Box 8506
Silver Spring, MD 20907
202-638-1320

Child Help U.S.A.
1345 El Centro Avenue
Hollywood, CA 90028
800-422-4453

"Exercise is work, but it's also pleasure, and pleasure is the part that keeps us at it."

The Latest Word in Sports Fitness

This chapter is devoted to you, the caregiver. I've discussed how Kinergetics will help enhance your baby's early months. Now I want to tell you how Kinergetics can also help you to improve your own fitness.

In the 1990's, scientific research caught up with the fitness craze. Many previously held notions of proper exercise procedures are now seen as myth. Today more realistic guidelines are being set.

Exercise physiologist William Haskell of Stanford University's School of Medicine has done research which concludes that short workouts (ten minutes) have similar beneficial effects to longer ones (twenty minutes or more) in stimulating the body's metabolic rate and increasing oxygen uptake and blood flow. These short duration spurts of activity may also help reduce injuries or fatigue. If you are too busy to exercise for long periods of time, exercise can be much more accessible when your program is divided into shorter, more manageable time periods.

Research is also demonstrating that checking your pulse to find your "target heart rate" is unnecessary for a number of reasons. Let's face it, who likes struggling with calculations of age, plus or minus this and divided by that as they're dripping with sweat and trying to regain their breath and composure? Inaccuracy is the principal reason for debunking this practice. Some people miscalculate the beats while checking their pulse, others can't locate it quickly enough before the pulse changes. Outside factors such as heat, humidity, altitude, and even stress, can greatly alter the pulse rate, making a reliable reading doubtful.

The American College of Sports Medicine has developed an alternative to pulse reading called the "perceived-exertion scale" (PES). How hard you feel you are exercising is the check point. The response is on a scale from zero to ten. Ten indicates maximum exertion with collapse inevitable, three is moderate exertion, while five equals strong intensity, and seven very strong. This method is far less complicated than the old target heart rate system. It requires nothing more difficult than being aware of your efforts — if you can't talk easily while doing the exercise it's time to slow down.

Current research also tells us to eliminate stretching before workouts. More muscles get torn or pulled because they have not been warmed up sufficiently before the demand to be flexible is placed upon them. Your muscles can be warmed up by the Tai Chi moves explained and illustrated in this book, or any gentle, slow exercise, such as walking or cycling for five minutes. A warmed-up muscle is able to absorb more force and is therefore less likely to tear. It is only after this attention toward properly preparing your muscles that you should intensify the dance routine.

Stretching is recommended and most advantageous when done following a period of elevated activity. Slow stretching after the workout, when muscles are tired, may help a muscle reduce any tendency to tighten up excessively to the point of spasm or soreness. Carefully read the chapter on stretching and study the illustrations. This will avoid faulty technique which can also contribute to injury.

So, it's the easy way to fitness these days, say the experts. Stretching before workouts isn't mandatory, nor is pulse taking. And if you're under time constraints (as caregivers often are), try to get in a ten minute workout on a regular basis. Dr. James G. Garrick, director of the Sports Medicine Center at St. Francis Hospital in San Francisco, California, stresses the need for all participants involved in a sports program to "avoid a cavalier attitude and aim for consistency" with regard to the time devoted to a workout.

Kinergetics fills the prescription for a wholesome fitness routine perfectly. It incorporates sound warm-up techniques, a low-impact aerobic workout which includes weight resistance for added benefits, and a complete list of stretches for cool-down times and proper back care. The short duration workouts are ideally suited to both a baby's shorter attention span and your need for a convenient and less time consuming exercise program. Remember, to gain the most out of your efforts just keep up the good work. Following a regular, consistent exercise routine is your best bet.

RESOURCES

BOOKS

Pregnancy and Sports Fitness, by Lynne Pirie (Arizona: Fisher Books, 1987).

Jane Fonda's Workout Books for Pregnancy, Birth and Recovery, by Femmy DeLyser (New York: Simon and Schuster, 1982).

MAGAZINES

Women's Sports and Fitness, P.O. Box 472, Mt. Morris, IL 61054-9908

ORGANIZATIONS

Women's Sports Foundation
342 Madison Avenue, Ste. 728
New York, NY 10017

American Fitness Association
P.O. Box 401
Durango, CO 81301
303-247-4109

Aerobics International Research Society
12330 Preston Rd.
Dallas, TX 75230
214-701-8001

"If people took care of their backs—if they got the proper exercise and avoided the foolish habits that place undue stress on the human back—they would spare themselves a great deal of pain and expense."

Reprinted with permission. © by James H. Sammons. *The American Medical Association Book of Back Care* (Preface). New York: Random House (1982).

CHAPTER 9

The Necessary Know-How of Back Care

From the top of the cervical spine at the base of the skull to the tip of the coccyx at the end of the "tail-bone," your spine is an intricate system of connecting bones (vertebrae). Between these vertebrae are nerves, ligaments, discs filled with fluid, and a number of large and small muscles that support the back. Most backaches occur in the lumbar region of the lower back, where the largest natural curve exists. This area is less flexible than the thoracic (mid-spine) area and has more demands on it than the cervical, upper back portion of the spine. These five lumbar vertebrae are the largest of the spine and function to support most weight bearing demands. Consequently they are apt to be strained by inefficient lifting, bending, and twisting.

There are many elements that contribute to back muscle strain and tension, such as stress, excess weight, improper posture, and overuse of insufficiently conditioned muscles. Obesity and poor posture cause improper spinal alignment. Such minor moves as simply bending over to pick up a baby's toy can lead to muscle spasms by irritating weak back muscles. A potential trouble-making posture is one that people rely on all too frequently, the use of a protruding hip to support a baby. Sometimes the habitual use of such an exaggerated one-sided placement causes misalignment and pain. The resulting discomfort can be aggravated by, and occur more often because of, the recent childbearing experience. Stress also can induce chronic shortening and tightening of muscles, perhaps triggering muscle spasms. When back problems manifest in this way it can over-stretch ligaments and overburden the spine, making it more susceptible to injury. These spasms or continued muscular contractions serve to protect your back from further damage and warn you of impending problems.

A strong and resilient back is able to withstand the many jolts it receives every day and is capable of supporting far greater weight than that of a baby or toddler. Yet many of us suffer back pain. As a parent of a new child, or a caregiver of babies and toddlers, your back has great demands placed on it daily. Proper posture and exercise can prevent most muscular back discomfort. One university study showed eighty-three percent of back pain was caused by weak or tense muscles. Kinergetics is meant to aid you in finding the most advantageous ways in which to hold your infant and to stimulate your desire to strengthen your back with exercises and stretching that provide stamina to the muscles most in demand with this weight bearing.

To minimize any propensity toward backaches it is important to maintain ideal body weight. The post-natal woman must try to regain her pre-pregnancy weight to relieve this possibility. The weight gain associated with pregnancy, or any "pot belly" over-weight condition brings with it the tendency to mis-align the body's natural center of gravity. An excessive curve develops in the lumbar region as it is pulled forward, compromising the vertebrae.

Poor posture adds undue stress on the spine. When properly aligned the spine will curve gently inward at the neck and lower back, and outward in the area of the ribcage, keeping the head, chest, and pelvis in a line above one another. When an extreme arch occurs in the lower back or shoulders are hunched over, weight imbalances result and strain is the by-product. The discs between the vertebrae are likely to be hurt when their space starts to narrow under this strain.

Exercise benefits spinal discs by contributing to the flow of nutrients. As John Jerome, an author specializing in the physiology of athletics, writes in *Staying Supple*, "The spinal fluids have no circulatory pump: the only circulation they get comes from movement." Kinergetics will force the vertebrae into action, opening up their joints inciting the flow of spinal and synovial fluids. If you do not follow a regular fitness routine, and opt to only exercise occasionally, your back may not be fit enough. If this is the case, you would be wise to incorporate back strengthening exercises into your daily regimen.

If you are susceptible to back problems you should seek the advice of your doctor before engaging in any activity that demands lifting, twisting, quick sudden movements, or excessive arching of the spine.

Sports such as golf, tennis, bowling, and racquetball are examples of high-risk activities if your back is weak. Except for minimal, short-duration lifting of your baby, Kinergetics avoids these potentially problematic moves. You must, for proper back care, follow all instructions accompanying the illustrations. There are some moves that are commonly done which can produce injury—like twisting your torso—that Kinergetics does not recommend. Please avoid twisting while dancing with your baby. You will jeopardize your back's integrity and the added weight will increase the risk of injury.

Sitting all day can have deleterious effects on the back, and is made worse if sitting is done improperly. Do not slump while sitting; look for well designed chairs if you sit for long periods of time. More pressure is exerted on the spine while sitting than while standing. So stand up, hold your baby, turn on the music, and get your feet moving.

As a parent or caregiver you are called upon to do lots of lifting of little ones. The simple act of bending your knees while lifting can relieve a lot of pressure on the spine. Nearly 300 extra pounds of stress on the spine is felt when knees are not bent. Always lift your child slowly and carefully bringing her close to your center of gravity (waist level).

If back complications arise for any reason, two days rest should be sufficient to relieve the problem. **Under no circumstances should you exercise if you are in pain.** Pain is quite different than the occasional achy feeling you can get after exercising vigorously. If the pain is gone, follow this short rest period with gentle stretching and pressure on the nerves should subside. With early intervention of rest followed by stretching it is often possible to avert back problems. The stretches in this book will strengthen your back and be helpful in your search for an effective defense against the majority of back injuries. Most beneficial will be the sitting abdominals and the dog pose. (Please refer to chapter 13, illustrations 29, 30, 33, and a variation of 26 which would have the legs outstretched at an angle, holding the leg position or slowly lowering them to the floor.)

If severe pain continues for longer than two days, see a doctor. Other exercises beneficial to those with back concerns are walking, swimming (back and crawl strokes), cross-country skiing, and cycling in an upright position.

With any good fitness program, conditioning should occur gradually. In weight-training especially, working out with small incremental weight increases over time is suggested. Another side benefit of Kinergetics is that babies provide for this progressive strengthening program by slowly gaining weight as they grow. It is to your physical advantage to start as early as possible with your baby, at about three months or as soon as they gain head control.

Please remember to wear proper shoes with good support while doing these exercises. Do your workout on a surface that is resilient enough to cushion the shock, such as a rug.

RESOURCES

BOOKS

The American Medical Association Book of Backcare, by Marion Steinmann (New York: Random House, 1982).

How To Take Care of Your Back, by Hugo A. Keim (Englewood Cliffs, NJ: Prentice-Hall, 1981).

ORGANIZATIONS

American Chiropractic Association
1701 Clarendon Blvd.
Arlington, VA 22209
212-276-8800

American College of Chiropractic Orthopedists
c/o Philip D. Rake, D.C.
1030 Broadway, Ste. 101
El Centro, CA 92243
619-352-1452

"Indeed a dance still lingers always at the heart of music and even the heart of the composer. Mozart, who was himself an accomplished dancer, used often to say, so his wife stated, that it was dancing, not music, that he really cared for."

"While culture evidently shapes the particular tempo of kinesic and linguistic behavior, it is "nature and nurture"—the experience of infancy—which instills the rhythm of life."

CHAPTER 10

Now for the Exercise

This workout offers the mother, father, or caregiver a collective fitness program. Warm-ups and cool-downs incorporate yoga, stretching, Tai Chi inspired moves, and back strengthening exercises, while the main portion of the program includes low-impact aerobics, weight-lifting principles, and varied dance moves.

Tai Chi has been practiced in China since ancient times. It is a form of exercise performed in a slow-motion manner with a meditative quality. Doctors of Chinese medicine often refer to a life force, or vital energy called "chi," which flows through the body on specific pathways. Tai Chi is believed to open these pathways allowing this vital energy to flow freely, in balance and harmony through the body, aiding the proper functioning of our internal organs and thus keeping the body strong and healthy.

The practice of yoga postures are believed to keep the body healthy, strong, and in harmony with nature, while bringing steadiness, lightness of limb, and evenness of mind. Many of the stretches suggested in this book are common to yoga postures, and may be familiar to you already.

Warming up and cooling down with Tai Chi and yoga improves balance, flexibility, coordination, concentration, and muscle tone. The warm-up time provides essential preparation for the more demanding aerobic dance to follow. A minimum of five minutes of warm-up for every twenty minutes of aerobic activity is best. Warm-up can be done with your baby, as is illustrated in a later chapter, or alone by jogging in place, by using a stationary bike or rowing machine, or any other similar exercise that slowly elevates your body temperature.

Before you pick up your baby to begin this activity, loosen up your arms by gently going through their natural range of motion. Rotate your arm from the shoulder joint in all possible directions, reaching up and down, in front and back, across your chest and in a circular motion. The flexing and warming of these muscles relaxes them before they go into their peak activity of lengthening and contracting. Any warm-up routine can be repeated after the main exercise segment is completed to help your body return to a resting state. Adding the specific arm stretches shown and described in chapter 13, illustrations 34, 35, and 36, will complement the range of motion exercises, offering a more intense stretch that serves to isolate the shoulder area more. The cool-down portion is the time to stretch more vigorously.

Most people know that to gain more physical "get up and go," exercise is indispensable. Getting your blood pumping oxygen throughout your body will increase your level of stamina and alertness. Proper breathing is also vital. Muscles become fatigued and are susceptible to injury when the amount of oxygen being delivered is insufficient.

How you breathe while exercising has an effect on your body. You must avoid the tendency to hold your breath while doing these movements, since the resulting lack of oxygen will weaken your ability to move with ease. Breathe out during contraction movements and inhale during expansive movements. Generally, you will find that you naturally inhale when you lift your baby or stretch. However, make no attempt to co-ordinate breathing when doing the Tai Chi form. Tai Chi movements are slow enough and less strenuous than stretching or dance moves. Your breathing will become deeper without conscious effort after doing the Tai Chi warm-ups for a few minutes.

Your muscles will contract as you alternately lift and lower your baby. Lifting and lowering, like other moves in Kinergetics, are repeated until the muscle group is tired or your baby shows that it is time to change the routine. Beware of any move that places the weight you are lifting away from your center of gravity and not in close contact with your body. Such moves must be done cautiously and only intermittently, with knees bent and no arching of the spine. Depending on the weight of the child, this can pose a certain risk, especially to those with a history of back problems. You can still develop muscle tone doing safer carriages that keep the baby's weight closer to your own body. The instructions which accompany the baby carriage illustrations reiterate this point and should always be kept in mind.

The best way to reform your body's dimensions is through weight-lifting, and that is exactly what you do every time you pick up your growing infant. By the time your baby is ten to twelve months of age, you may be lifting twenty or more pounds. This upper-body conditioning is also a valuable training exercise for other sports.

It is important to take great care during the transition from one move to the next. For example, if you are embracing your baby close to your heart and want to turn her around to face outwards, move carefully and gracefully, with controlled stretching.

ALWAYS CONSULT WITH YOUR DOCTOR BEFORE ENGAGING IN ANY NEW EXERCISE PROGRAM, NO MATTER HOW FIT YOU FEEL YOU ARE!

Keep in mind the basic rule of dance as you do these movements: be focused, be aware of your body before you begin to move, and have each part of your body properly aligned. Whether an activity calls for a static (motionless stretch) or a dynamic (moving) placement, proper body alignment is essential at all times. Your head, neck, and shoulders should be in a straight line and have adequate spacing between them; avoid bringing your shoulders too close to your ears as this constricting effect causes undue muscle tension.

Kinergetics is something you can do as a complete exercise routine, given the willingness of your little one, or as part of your over-all exercise program. Ideally, for maximum aerobic benefit, you should try for two or three, twenty to thirty minute workouts a week, plus the recommended warm-up and cool-down time. These twenty or thirty minute workouts can be broken into shorter ten minute segments repeated two or three times during the day.

RESOURCES

BOOKS

The Jazzersize Workout Book, by Judi Sheppard Missett (New York: Charles Scribner's Sons, 1986).

Soft Workouts: Low Impact Exercise, by Time-Life (Alexandria, VA: Time-Life Books, 1988).

Non Impact Aerobics—The NIA Technique, by Debbie Rosas and Carlos Rosas (New York: Avon Books, 1987).

The New Aerobics For Women, by Kenneth H. Cooper (New York: Bantam, 1988).

ORGANIZATIONS

Aerobics and Fitness Foundation of America
15250 Ventura Blvd., Ste. 310
Sherman Oaks, CA 91403
818-905-0040

"Perhaps the healthiest way of dealing with products of another culture is to recognize ways in which they can improve our own."

© by Herman Kauz. *Tai Chi Handbook* (page 13). Garden City, New York: Dolphin Books, Doubleday (1974).

CHAPTER 11

Warm-Up with Tai Chi

Often called "Taoist calisthenics," Tai Chi was designed from practical experimentation with anatomy, physiology, and body mechanics. These gentle movements do provide enough stimulation of the muscles to be considered exercise.

In order to prevent strain with any move, Tai Chi involves constantly shifting one's weight in a slow moving form. This principle of continuous flowing movement comes as a great benefit to those who are called upon to continually hold a baby for sometimes long periods. By shifting our weight we lessen the burden of placing all the weight of the baby on any one body part. Since our arms will be holding the baby in various positions, only leg forms are performed. This is where Kinergetics adapts this Eastern form of exercise to suit our caregiving needs.

To perform Tai Chi correctly one should be as relaxed as possible. Focus on each movement of the body and move as slowly and steadily as possible.

Breathing should be easy and natural, through the nose. Because bent knees are a perpetual part of all moves, Tai Chi puts a significant amount of demand on the leg muscles; standing fully erect occurs only when the form is completed. As you improve the technique you will be able to sink lower into a distinct "quarter-squat" form. Take shorter steps, coordinating the end motion of each step with the beginning of the next one. Make the action soft, gentle, and continuous. Avoid performing the same isolated movement over and over again.

Proper alignment is always important. With Tai Chi, the head, neck and spine must be in line, with a straight back and torso (relaxed, not rigid). The knee of the forward leg should not go beyond the toes of the foot. Feet are placed slowly and deliberately in position. On forward movements the feet come down heel first. On backward steps the toes descend first (except where otherwise noted). Firmly establish balance on one foot prior to lifting the other foot to take a step. Generally, weight is more predominantly on one foot, not on both except for preparation or completion of moves.

Your feet act to "root" you as the energy being created passes through your legs. Control is in the waist. When we add a child and perform Tai Chi together, cradling the baby at our center of gravity— waist level, they serve to remind us of what practitioners of Tai Chi call our control center. This is the area of the body, around our navel, from which they believe all our body's energy radiates—the source of all major body movements.

This ancient exercise practice helps us remember the Chinese concept of opposites, or yin/yang philosophy. When there is a movement upward there must follow a downward motion; likewise when there is a forward move, there should follow a backward one; and when there is a move to the left, there must be one to the right. The philosophy teaches followers to avoid extremes, to maintain physical and mental balance, and to seek to live in harmony with the powerful forces in the world.

Illustrations 1 through 7 show Tai Chi movements to be done as a series of moves.

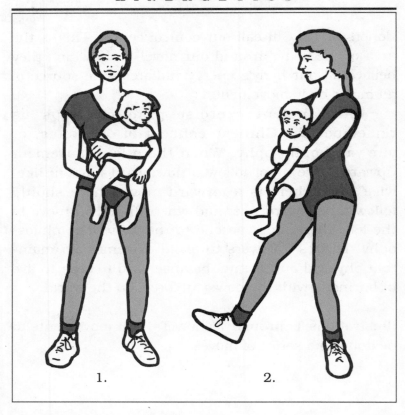

1.   2.

Illustration #1. Feet are parallel, spaced about twelve inches apart, and aligned under each shoulder. Knees should be slightly bent.

Illustration #2. Bend the left knee a little more while shifting most of your weight to your left foot. Turn your right foot directly right. Rotate the baby as your right foot turns, in one smooth motion along with your head, shoulders, and hips.

3.   4.

Illustration #3. Shift all your weight to your right foot. Your left heel should leave the ground. The right knee should be bent. Maintain baby and body position.

Illustration #4. Just prior to shifting your weight completely on your right foot, begin to turn your body counterclockwise (left). Now step north, straight out with your left foot in the direction it was pointing, placing the heel on the floor first.

Illustration #5. About seventy percent of your weight should now be transferred to your left foot; continue to rotate your body and baby to the left. Before conclusion of the weight transfer, rotate your body so that baby and you are facing directly north. Also, your right toe turns inward forty-five degrees (northeast).

Illustration #6. Continue the shifting of weight to your left foot, while your right heel rises.

7.

Illustration #7. When weight is almost entirely on your left foot, start to rotate your body slightly clockwise (right). With one hundred percent of your weight on your left foot, raise your right foot and put the heel where the toe was. Shift your weight so that it is evenly distributed between both feet. Turn each foot so that it is in the beginning position, only spaced further apart. You can continue to close the space to the distance of twelve inches by placing all your weight on one of your feet and drawing in the opposite leg. Again, all your weight is evenly distributed.

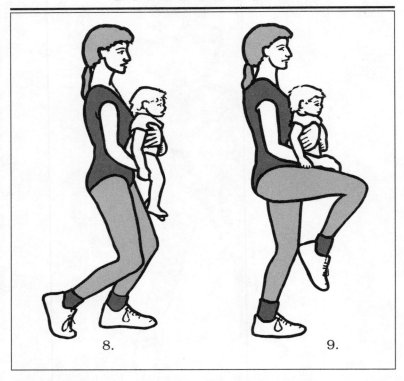

8.   9.

Illustration #8. With a slightly narrower stance use the beginning position to incorporate the following two illustrations, known as the "Golden Cock Stands on One Leg." Place one hundred percent of your weight on your left foot with knees bent. Your right foot is placed toes down, heels up behind you.

Illustration #9. Bring your right foot forward and continue the movement by raising your right knee in front of you to waist level. Return to beginning position and repeat raising other knee.

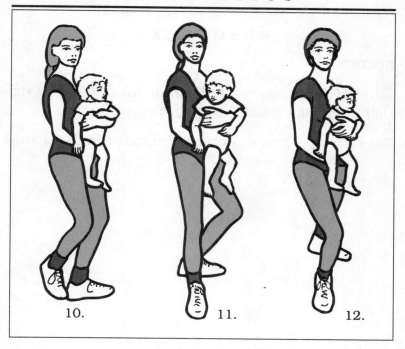

10.   11.   12.

Illustration #10. While doing the previous movement, "Golden Cock Stands on One Leg," you can incorporate the "Brush Knee" move. Do this by bringing in your left foot to your right knee.

Illustration #11. Step forward and to the left with your left foot and place it down, heel first.

Illustration #12. As you place the rest of your foot down, shift seventy percent of your weight to it. (To get back to a starting position, so as to continue the movement using the other side, rotate hips, waist, baby, right leg and foot counterclockwise to the starting position).

RESOURCES

BOOKS

Tai Chi Handbook, by Herman Kauz (New York: Dolphin Books, Doubleday, 1974).

Tai Chi, by Danny Connor (London: Stanley Paul, 1989).

"The baby who is held closely, cuddled, caressed, and treated as nearly as possible as he was treated when he was still in the womb is reassured. After what he may well have experienced as the trauma of birth, he comes once more into safe harbor in the reassuring arms of a loving mother. This kind of communication, the message of reassurance, is of the utmost significance to the baby."

Reprinted with permission. © by Dr. Ashley Montagu. *The Human Connection* (page 95). New York: McGraw-Hill (1979).

CHAPTER 12

Dance Steps and Carriages for Baby

Kinergetics is intended to be a soft, low-impact, workout. Soft workouts reduce the shock and force of taking off and landing that is associated with high-impact activities such as running and high-impact aerobic dance. Such jarring sports can injure your joints, muscles, and ligaments. It is much safer to workout with minimal irritation to your body. By using movements that allow you to keep one foot in contact with the floor at all times and to exercise on a resilient surface, you eliminate many of these dangers.

Aerobic capacity is measured by the efficiency of your cardiovascular system to extract oxygen from air and deliver it to working muscles for fuel. An efficient cardiovascular system improves your oxygen consumption. Building cardiovascular endurance is possible when an exercise employs large muscle groups and is continuously performed commensurate with your fitness level, thus keeping the demand for oxygen high.

Weight-bearing exercises like Kinergetics, which place mechanical stress on the bones, can actually help to strengthen bone composition and slow down osteoporosis. It will aid the circulatory system as well.

IF YOU HAVE A HISTORY OF HIGH BLOOD PRESSURE, WEIGHT-BEARING EXERCISE MAY BE CONTRA-INDICATED. PLEASE SEEK THE ADVICE OF YOUR DOCTOR BEFORE ENGAGING IN THIS ACTIVITY.

Eventually children reach the state where they equate music with dance. They love it—it's infectious. To dance about with happy loving people surely must be heavenly.

After the first year, when babies become more of a physical burden to lift continually, they become engrossed in their developing motor skills. But beware, when the music comes on, you may get many requests for dances. If that is the case, watch your back, and limit the time engaged in this activity. When my daughter, Cara, was two years old she always invited me to dance with her, and I graciously accepted for a song or two. Now that my children are older the requests keep coming, but dancing Kinergetics style is only sporadically introduced in between the classical ballet moves or swing-style bop steps we entwine each other with.

A child's weight does limit the safe and sensible execution of Kinergetics, but it is convenient that our babies increase their weight gradually, giving our bodies time to adjust to the heavier load. In technical fitness jargon, this technique is referred to as "progressive overload."

As I have indicated, you can create your own routine of moves, using music of your choice. Plan to workout at a time when you and your baby are most receptive, perhaps in the morning, or after a nap. Avoid exercising immediately after a meal—that goes for both you and your baby. Wear loose clothing that allows freedom of movement, or a leotard and tights, which are ideal for keeping muscles warm.

You will want to take into account individual differences in the capabilities and interests of babies. A ten month old may enjoy a ride atop your shoulders, whereas a three month old would feel too insecure. Most of the moves are intended for use with babies who already demonstrate neck and head control. Be aware of the strengths of your baby.

The commentary with the illustrations indicates the appropriate stage of development at which to introduce a particular carriage. Remember, this is not meant to be a formal, structured program that emphasizes the activity over the needs and wishes of your baby. Overstimulation can be prevented by using softer music and cradling or over-the-shoulder embraces. Your baby's own involvement and mood will dictate the moves you do.

WARNINGS FOR YOUR BABY:

ALWAYS SUPPORT HEAD AND NECK UNTIL IT IS VERY CLEAR THAT SHE HAS COMPLETE CONTROL (APPROXIMATELY 3–4 MONTHS).

AVOID ANY QUICK, JERKY, OR SUDDEN MOVEMENTS. NEVER SHAKE OR RATTLE YOUR INFANT.

CONSULT YOUR BABY'S DOCTOR FOR APPROVAL TO PARTICIPATE IN THIS ACTIVITY.

ALL SPECIAL NEEDS CHILDREN MUST HAVE CONSENT OF THEIR DOCTOR.

PREMATURE BABIES, OR INFANTS WITH SEIZURE DISORDERS OR HEART PROBLEMS, MUST SEEK THE APPROVAL OF THEIR DOCTOR TO PARTICIPATE IN THIS ACTIVITY AND MUST DO SO IN A VERY MODIFIED WAY.

The dance steps you use can be your own personal mixture of the aerobic steps suggested below, and any way you move your feet in dance that may be familiar to you. Your footwork does not have to follow any set routine. If you know tap dancing steps, incorporate those into your workout. Some of you may know ballet and will enjoy doing the five different feet positions, adding a plie now and then. Still others of you may know jazz, modern, or ethnic dance steps. Feel free to do whatever combination of steps feels right for you. I enjoy "contra" or "buck" dancing to country music at times. (People from the south will know what I'm talking about.) Whatever you choose, just keep those feet moving and be conscious of the way in which you are holding your baby.

The following dance steps are common to low-impact aerobics.

1. You can simulate jogging in place on the balls of your feet, but keep one or both feet in contact with the floor to ensure a low-impact aerobic workout. Feet should be shoulder width apart.

2. Variation of #1: Use a heel tap shuffle from right to left foot.

3. Variation of #2: Feet alternate with a forward motion having the heel shuffle land eight to ten inches in front of you.

4. Feet shoulder width apart, tap the toe of one foot behind the other and alternate to opposite foot.

5. From the starting position of two feet slightly bent at the knees shoulder width apart and weight easily on balls of feet, kick lightly in front of you, alternating legs.

6. Variation of #5 would be a kick directed across the body, alternating legs.

7. Another variation of the above would be taking turns with each foot kicking to the side twelve inches or so and then wider— up to eighteen inches.

8. You can exaggerate step #1, jogging in place, with a more pronounced bent knee kick behind you, one leg at a time with foot off the ground at least a foot and heading towards your buttocks.

9. A variation on #8: With knees staying in front of you and lifting waist high.

10. Vary #9 with more of an across the body knee to the waist level move.

11. All these moves can be tried with legs spread slightly further apart.

12. In this wider stance you can more easily isolate the movement of your hips. Shift to one side and follow with the hip, raising on the balls of your weighted foot, and alternate to the other side. Repeat as you see fit.

13. Use the length of the room to sashay along with whatever moves feel good. You can skip, step side to side, do crossovers with one foot alternating in front and then behind. You get the idea, now be creative.

When you add your baby to these common low-impact aerobic dance moves you will beat any boredom from repeating them. Changing the way in which you carry your child demands quite a workout for the arms and coordinating these moves with simple basic steps makes for an adequate conditioning routine. The carriages used in Kinergetics are illustrated in the following pages. Please pay close attention to the instructions.

13.

OVER THE HEART EMBRACE

Illustration #13. The most common way to hold a baby. Especially suitable for the very young infant. Good for eye-to-eye contact, important to incorporate often to check baby's responsiveness. Most useful with slower tempo movements, in beginning or ending a dance, and when baby begins to reach their particular stimulus threshold.

*Keep knees slightly bent.

*With baby facing toward you place one arm supporting buttocks and the other around babies back. Hold baby over your heart.

*Keep baby close to your body.

*Stand erect, watch lower curvature of spine.

*Be relaxed, allow neck, head, and shoulders not to be hunched over or crowded together.

14.

OUTWARD FACING CHAIR CARRIAGE

Illustration #14. This pose is quite popular with babies, it gives infants an opportunity to see their surroundings in a comfortable and secure hold. This is the most basic carriage used in Kinergetics. It is especially suitable for warm-up with Tai Chi.

*Hold baby facing outwards.

*The weight of baby should be mostly on your forearm which is supporting baby's bottom, your other arm acts to support baby's upper torso at their waist level.

*Remember to alternate arms used as main support.

*Baby is carried comfortably at waist high level.

*The caregiver's arms may rock baby in a side to side swaying motion or remain centered as feet movements dictate.

15.

WAIST HIGH, TWO HANDED
OUTWARD FACING HOLD

Illustration #15. This adds variety and movement for both caregiver and baby. Baby is held higher up, as its bottom is waist high, which brings the baby's face close to the caregiver's.

*Provides the opportunity to talk to baby, whispering sweet somethings into their ears.

*Good workout for arms which carry the weight equally.

*Arm movements can be up and down or slightly to the side.

*Keep infant close to your body.

*Especially suitable for foot movements that incorporate knee raises.

16.

RESTING ON CHEST, OUTWARD FACING
TWO HANDED HOLD

Illustration #16. A good transitional hold following the waist high outward facing two handed hold. Allows some of the infant's weight to be carried by caregiver's chest. Creates a subtle movement for baby altering their vantage point to a higher level. Try kissing baby's back for added fun.

*Hold baby securely with two hands around their waist.

*Keep baby close to your body and centered.

*Your hands, arms, and shoulders are at work with this move carrying the majority of the weight.

*Keep shoulders relaxed and well back, away from your ears, allowing the muscles in action to do their job comfortably.

17.

FACE TO FACE, TWO HANDED HOLD

Illustration #17. This movement requires a degree of care for the adult participant if the baby seems at all heavy. Any hold where baby is not close to your body and is raised above head level creates more demand on your back.

*Use with caution.

*Keep knees bent and allow quadricep muscles of upper thighs to accept some burden of the weight.

*The baby is held with both hands and arms with weight equally distributed.

*This is a useful carriage for checking baby's enthusiasm, eye to eye contact provides the means and adds extra stimulation.

*Avoid excessive arching of the lower back.

*Feet should be comfortably spaced to allow for a good foundation in supporting baby's weight.

*Baby can be moved up and down which will provide your arm muscles a wonderful toning workout.

*If baby is moved side to side be sure to do so by means of using your entire body, torso, legs and arms; do not isolate your arm movements to the side while keeping the rest of your body aligned straight ahead.

18.

UP HIGH IN THE SKY HOLD

Illustration #18. This is more a movement than a hold. This is so commonly done and provides fun eye-to-eye contact and real excitement for baby that it has its place in some dances. But, BEWARE *USE WITH CAUTION* depending on the weight of your baby this is a potentially dangerous move for sensitive backs.

*Use infrequently and only for very short periods of time.

*Always bend knees and let upper legs do much to help support the weight.

*Keep feet spaced about shoulder width apart.

*Watch for excessive arching of back.

19.

FLY LIKE A BIRD HOLD

Illustration #19. This is fun, but prolonged use at any one time may over-stimulate some babies. Always check with baby for a reaction with a face-to-face hold. Babies will often vocally sound out their approval. Good to use slowly and gently. Useful to pat baby's tummy to relieve gas. This is a very active movement for both participants and should be done after proper warm-up time for both of you.

*Get into this position by first placing baby in the waist high facing outward position.

*Baby is supported with one arm under the entire length of their torso while the other forearm and hand supports the neck and shoulders.

*Keep baby close to your body and waist level, knees bent.

*Avoid twisting motion.

*Motion of flying can be simulated by rocking legs and swaying arms either slowly or a bit quicker.

20.

PONY RIDE HOLD

Illustration #20. This movement offers a good stretch for the legs and a momentary break for your arms. For young babies secure with two hands. Take note to align your body correctly when executing this move.

*Begin by standing, spread legs apart four to four and a half feet. Hold the baby facing outwards at waist level. The left leg should be turned ninety degrees to the left while the right foot is only slightly turned towards the left. Keep right leg outstretched and knee nearly locked. You will be stretching the right leg hamstring muscles. Now bend the left knee until the thigh is parallel to the floor. The left shin should be directly under the knee in a straight perpendicular line to the floor, creating a right angle between the left thigh and calf. Rotate slowly and place baby on knee.

*Do not extend left knee past the ankle.

*Hold for twenty or thirty seconds.

*Slowly bring baby back towards your midsection and slowly again straighten the bent knee, rotate the foot back to starting position. You should be back to your four foot wide stance.

*Repeat bending opposite knee.

21.

ROCK-A-BYE BABY CRADLE HOLD

Illustration #21. Everyone is familiar with cradling their baby. Cup one hand under baby's bottom and the other supporting baby's upper back, shoulder, and neck.

*Good for eye-to-eye contact and assessing baby's mood.

*Best used with slow tempo music.

*You can gently rock baby back and forth with the use of your arms, hips, and legs.

*AVOID TWISTING MOTION as it may cause back complications.

*Keep baby close to body, do not extend arms out straight.

*Avoid fast or bouncy foot movements while holding baby in this carriage, as it often makes baby feel less secure.

22.

THE COMMON HIP RIDE

Illustration #22. Everyone does it, it is convenient for freeing up a hand for any number of reasons. But be aware that this common way of carrying baby is not friendly to your back.

*LIMIT USE AND BE SURE TO USE BOTH HIPS EQUALLY.

*Baby must have gained adequate back, neck, and head strength to help support a safe and upright posture.

*Support baby with your hip and your arm around their back at their waist level.

*Good for limited use to loosen up arms and to put them through some range of motion; stretch them out in all directions and rotations.

*Repeat using opposite hip and arm.

23.

FIREMAN'S SHOULDER CARRY

Illustration #23. Baby must have gained adequate strength to safely sit upon your shoulders and neck area. Either support baby with hands as shown or with open hands around baby's upper torso, under their arms.

*CAUTION: FOR LIMITED USE ONLY. This means of carrying baby places a fair amount of strain on the caregiver and must be used infrequently and with caution!

*Begin with a "facing outward" carriage and slowly and carefully lift baby up and over your head and place upon your neck and shoulders.

*Older babies often get many laughs out of this one if they are ready for some more high-spirited play.

*Move feet about as desired. Go slow at first and listen and feel for signs of acceptance or rejection of movement.

24.

ONE ARM, FRONT FACING OUTWARD CARRY

Illustration #24. Baby must feel secure with only one arm supporting its midsection.

*Hold baby very close to your midline.

*Good for loosening up arms, rotating and stretching them in all directions.

*Remember to switch to opposite arms so both get relief.

RESOURCES

BOOKS

The Dance of Life, by Havelock Ellis (Westport, CT: Greenwood Press Publishers, 1973).

ORGANIZATIONS

The American Alliance for Health,
Physical Education, Recreation, and Dance
1900 Association Drive
Reston, VA 22091

"Both 'flexible' and 'supple,' says Webster's, describe the ability to bend or fold easily, 'without creases, cracks, breaks, or other injuries.' For an athletic body, that ought to be the minimum starting point."

© by John Jerome. *Staying Supple: The Bountiful Pleasures of Stretching* (page 11). New York: Bantam Books (1987).

Stretching It All Out

Stretching following a workout is always an excellent idea since your muscles will be warm and receptive. Good flexibility allows for soft tissue to maintain its most efficient length and for the joints to remain lubricated. Muscular resistance to demands placed upon them are diminished with proper and timely stretching.

The usefulness of stretching can be felt throughout the whole body, despite the fact that flexibility is applied on a joint-by-joint basis. If you reach behind your head you call upon not only your shoulder muscles but your stomach muscles as well. This move is also dependent on the flexibility of your hip and spine.

To do any stretching efficiently your muscles must be relaxed. Your efforts will be effective in reducing injury, increasing performance, and reducing any soreness from your routine if you concentrate on regular stretching of the major joint areas.

Go easy on yourself. It is not necessary to force your muscles and tendons to stretch beyond the comfort range; they will progressively loosen as time goes on. Avoid bouncing or any prolonged holding of a stretch (more than twenty to thirty seconds). Slow, controlled moves with the feeling of relaxing ought to be your aim. Relax, elongate the muscles, and try to feel the stretch pull taut the elasticity of the tendons. Breathe deeply.

When we pay attention to the smaller muscles and connective tissue that support the larger calves and biceps and so forth, we aid in the proper alignment of our frame and joints. Many injuries are frequently felt by these supporting muscles and tissues. Avoiding these minor mishaps will be more probable if we direct our attention to the care and maintenance of connective tissue. Since any quick move can tear this connective tissue, keeping it supple is most important.

Connective tissue is the unifying thread that makes our body one flexible unit. Force from muscle power is transmitted via the network of connective tissue that holds muscle to bone, and ligaments which connect bones together. It is much more than tendons and ligaments, it is the array of fascia that makes up and stabilizes the fundamental structure and material of our organs, arterial walls, and musculature.

Our bodies are meant to work as one interconnected unit. A weak hip can cause overcompensation of the ankle resulting in chronic sprains, or Achilles tendinitis. Tendinitis is inflammation of the tendon and is a frequent sports injury complaint.

Protein based fiber makes up connective tissue. Collagen allows for tensile strength, while elastin offers elasticity to the tissue. Mucopolysaccharide provides lubrication to the fibers, and also acts as a cohesive bonding agent that keeps the tissue a collective mass. Proper stretching will allow for the efficient functioning of these various components, thereby decreasing the risk of injury.

Connective tissue is susceptible to both under- and over-use. Over-use injuries can heal, but do so slowly. Tendons have to move over joints, so it is true to say tendinitis is a joint related injury. When tendons are not flexible enough to move across joints they may tear or become inflamed. With underuse the structural components deteriorate, the tissue tightens as the collagen becomes stiff and the elastic frays and loses its elastic quality.

The following are illustrations of stretches to increase flexibility. Many of these you might have seen or done before. If not, the illustrations and instructions should be clear enough for you to understand how to perform each one successfully.

25.

Illustration #25. Lie on your back, lay baby belly down on your stomach, reach back behind head stretching as far as possible. You can hold baby with one hand while stretching the opposite one over your head, then switch to the other arm. Feel your body elongating from head to toes and heels. With both hands around baby slowly lift her up with outstretched arms creating a weight lifting exercise. Useful for cool down time.

*Very good arm workout.

*Affords good eye contact for added stimulation and a comfortable means of talking with baby.

26.

Illustration #26. Lie on your back with baby sitting on your midriff or abdomen and raise legs straight up in the air. Toes or heels can point straight up. To vary this stretch while in the same position, lower legs while straight up to more of a forty-five degree angle and hold this position for twenty seconds, keep a secure hold on baby. You can also slowly lower your legs providing a rocking motion for baby as well as a strong abdominal workout for you. Or, create a sit-up by carefully elevating your neck and shoulders off the floor.

*This is a fun time to tickle and talk to baby.

*You may also vary this by supporting baby with your hands while in this position allowing for your legs, while remaining stretched upward, to separate.

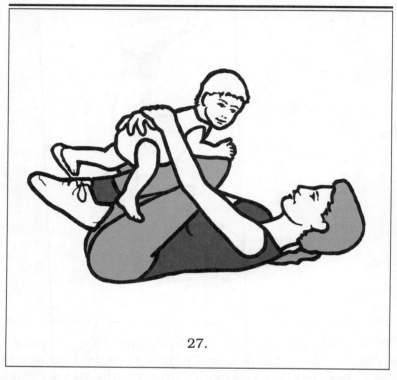

27.

Illustration #27. Lying flat on your back with legs out-stretched, bring knees to chest and place baby belly down on your lower legs, and wrap your arms around her. This move helps to relieve back tension. Variation on #27: Lying down draw one knee at a time into chest while keeping other leg outstretched; baby can be in same position.

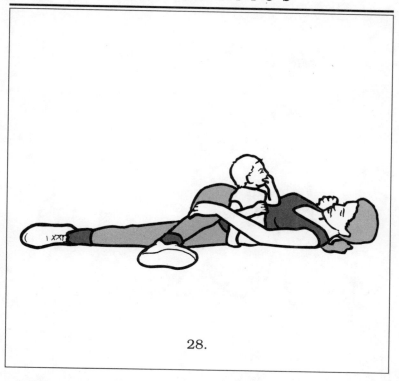

28.

Illustration #28. Baby needs to sit nestled next to your left upper torso as you lay backside down on floor, lift right leg ninety degrees, then place on floor to left side, creating a twisting of entire spine. Your right hip should be aligned on top of your left hip. Try to keep shoulders flat on floor, right arm outstretched. Keep adequate distance between ears and shoulders, elongating the space between them allows for ease of movement and relaxation of muscles; the head turns to the left. Switch to use opposite side. To increase spinal twist stretch, bend the knee of the leg you are crossing over.

29.

Illustration #29. Lie on your back with your legs out-stretched and bend your knees. Flatten your lower back to the floor. Place baby on your lap in a sitting position facing you and resting against your thighs—your arms reaching straight alongside your knees or helping to support baby if necessary. Now lift your shoulders and upper back. Hold for thirty seconds if possible to strengthen abdominal area and increase back fitness.

30.

Illustration #30. The following stretches demand that your baby be able to safely sit or lie on your stomach without your holding assistance. While in the same position as illustration 29, clasp hands behind your neck keeping arms next to your head or vary with elbows out to side.

31.

Illustration #31. A popular hamstring stretch begins in a sitting position with one leg outstretched while opposite leg is bent at the knee with foot inward toward crotch. Baby may be placed facing outwards, or inwards facing you, and close to your crotch for support. Relaxing your upper body, reach for your outstretched foot with both hands, or if baby needs support, use free hand. Repeat using opposite side. Vary this position by placing both legs straight out in front of you while sitting and then stretch from the waist, reaching for toes or baby.

32.

Illustration #32. Basic groin stretch begins in a similar sitting position with baby again close to your crotch, facing outwards. This time both knees are bent with both feet inwards meeting together in front of body at midline. Grasp your feet with both hands and with an imaginary downward push on your knees and a straight back, as if a string were pulling you from the top of your head, stretch the groin area. You can vary this a bit by having your feet placed further away from your crotch and simply bending forward at the waist creating a bit more of a stretch.

33.

Illustration #33. This pose looks like a dog stretching. Lie on the floor— stomach down. Baby will need to be in front of you lying or sitting. With the toes pointing back and feet one foot apart place hands on floor at waist level, fingers pointing towards head. Breathe in and raise the trunk as far back as possible. Try not to have knees touching floor. Keep legs straight and knees straightened. Feel the spine, calves and thighs stretch. The buttocks should be tightly contracted. The chest pushed forward, the neck elongates fully and allows the head to fall back. Allow for full extension in all these areas, including the back part of the arms. Breathe deep. Release stretch by bending the elbows and relax on the floor.

34.   35.

Illustrations #34 and #35. To loosen the shoulders efficiently you will need both hands free, so baby will need to
be happy just watching from some safe vantage point.
Start by standing upright and clasping your hands behind
your buttocks, arms should be straight with an intense
pull causing the breast to push upwards toward the
ceiling. Variation of #34: Retain the above pose and simply
bend forward at the waist bringing your arms comfortably
and slowly over your head. See illustration #35.

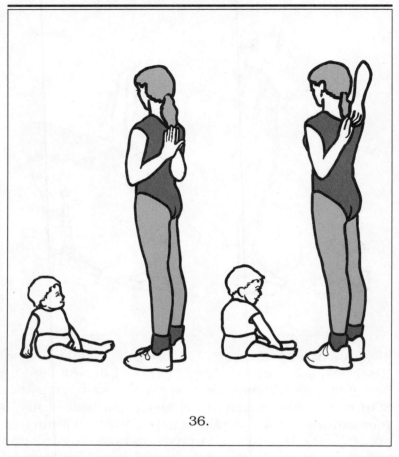

36.

Illustration #36. Another arm clasp begins again in a standing position with arms folded behind your back either by taking hold of the fingers or by folding arms with palms together in a prayer position, as illustrated. More stretch is provided by bringing the hands in prayer position up along spine as far as possible.

See illustration #20 - in the chapter on dance steps and carriages for baby. Standing, spread legs apart four to four and a half feet. Hold baby facing outwards at waist level. The right leg should be turned ninety degrees to the right while the left foot is only slightly turned towards the right, keep left leg outstretched and knee nearly locked. You will be stretching the left leg hamstring muscles. Now bend the right knee until the thigh is parallel to the floor. The right shin should be directly under the knee in a straight perpendicular line to the the floor, creating a right angle between the right thigh and calf. Place baby on knee. Do not extend right knee past the ankle. Hold for twenty seconds or so. Slowly bring baby back towards your midsection and slowly again straighten the bent knee, rotate the foot back to starting position. You should be back to your four foot wide stance. Repeat, bending opposite knee.

Those are some basic stretches that shouldn't require too much time to complete. Do what you can following a workout, and what you don't get to during one session, save for the next.

RESOURCES

BOOKS

Light on Yoga, by B.K.S. Iyengar (New York: Schocken Books, 1972).

Staying Supple, by John Jerome (New York: Bantam Books, 1987).

Lilia's Yoga and You, by Lilia M. Folan (New York: Bantam Books, 1972).

Yoga For Health, by Richard L. Hittleman (New York: Ballantine, 1983).

Gentle Yoga, by Lorna Bell and Eudora Seyfer (Berkelely, CA: Celestial Arts, 1987).

ORGANIZATIONS

Yoga Research Foundation
61 S.W. 74th Avenue
Miami, FL 33143
305-666-2006

"Laved by the amniotic fluid and caressed by the walls of the uterus to the symphonic beat of two hearts, the baby is already in tune with the deepest rhythms of existence. The dance of life has begun."

Reprinted with permission. © by Dr. Ashley Montagu. *Growing Young* (page 166). Massachusetts: Bergin and Garvey (1989).

CHAPTER 14

It All Adds Up

The ability to cope with the demands of everyday life depends upon the wellness of mind and body. Take good care of them. This exercise program will help you decrease anxiety, aid your parenting skills, increase self-esteem and personal satisfaction, and improve your ability to relax and to sleep. It also will act metabolically to increase fat metabolism, oxygen uptake, muscle mass, and glucose tolerance. Thus it will contribute to your overall wellness. Enjoy Kinergetics for your sake and your baby's.

Your new baby is a star shining for you. When you help her with an attitude of unconditional love and understanding, with patience, confidence, and warmth, you are helping to create a person who will learn to reciprocate with the same caring affection and appreciation for life. You are beginning now to share a bond that will be as deep as the effort with which you meet this budding relationship. You are a family, with much to gain and learn about yourselves and about life through the course of your mutually shared lives. I hope Kinergetics proves to be an invaluable experience for you and your baby.

Average Development of Large Motor Skills for Infants

(SOME BABIES' SEQUENCE OF DEVELOPMENT IN LOCOMOTION WILL BE EARLIER OR LATER THAN TIME FRAME INDICATED.)

6 weeks—while lying with face downward on stomach chin lifts off surface approximately 45 degrees. Shows rounded back while sitting. Head held up intermittently when sitting.

8 weeks—back still rounded. When lifted from a supine to a sitting position head drops back and lags behind, but not completely.

10–12 weeks—lying on stomach weight is now on forearms and face is nearly 90 degrees to surface.

12 weeks—infant begins to bear much of the weight when standing.

12–14 weeks—stands more erect.

16 weeks—no head lag.

11–20 weeks—becomes interested in hands.

12–16 weeks—while lying face upwards (supine) soles of feet come together. One foot is placed on opposite knee.

20 weeks—feet are brought to mouth, plays with feet. Lifts head from supine when about to be pulled up.

24 weeks—while lying on stomach weight is on hands with arms extended. Head lifts up spontaneously while supine. Objects are transferred from one hand to the other.

26 weeks—while sitting the hands are forward in front of body for support.

28 weeks—while standing, infant bears all weight. Sitting without support.

44 weeks—is able to turn around to pick up a toy without overbalancing.

52 weeks—walks without assistance.

60 weeks—kneels without help.

Parent Resources

AMERICAN ACADEMY OF PEDIATRICS (AAP)
141 Northwest Point Boulevard
P.O. Box 927
Elk Grove Village, IL
60009-0927
708-228-5005

NATIONAL ASSOCIATION FOR THE EDUCATION
OF YOUNG CHILDREN
1834 Connecticut Ave., NW
Washington, DC
20009-5786
202-232-8777

ASSOCIATION FOR CHILDHOOD EDUCATION
INTERNATIONAL (ACEI)
11501 Georgia Avenue, Suite 312
Wheaton, MD 20902
301-942-2443

BLACK CHILD DEVELOPMENT INSTITUTE
1028 Connecticut Avenue, NW
Washington, DC 20036
202-387-1281

CHILDREN'S DEFENSE FUND
122 C Street, NW
Washington, DC 20001
202-628-8787

INFANT DEVELOPMENT EDUCATION
ASSOCIATION (IDEA)
c/o Catherine H. Thompson, RN, MSN
Department of Education
Mary Washington Hospital
Fredericksburg, VA 22401
703-371-2712

LA LECHE LEAGUE
9616 Minneapolis Avenue
Box 1209
Franklin Park, IL
60131-8209
708-455-7730
800-LA-LECHE

FOUNDATION FOR CHILD DEVELOPMENT
345 East 46th Street
New York, NY 10017
212-697-3150

NATIONAL COMMITTEE FOR PREVENTION
OF CHILD ABUSE
332 South Michigan Avenue, Suite 1250
Chicago, IL 60604-4357
312-663-3520

THE AMERICAN HUMANE ASSOCIATION
Children's Division
63 Inverness Drive East
Englewood, CO 80220
303-792-9900

C. HENRY KEMPE NATIONAL CENTER
FOR THE PREVENTION AND TREATMENT
OF CHILD ABUSE AND NEGLECT
1205 Oneida Dr.
Denver, CO 80220
303-321-3963

PARENTS ANONYMOUS
6733 South Sepulveda Blvd., Suite 270
Los Angeles, CA 90045
In California: 213-388-6685
Outside of California: 800-421-0353

PARENTS WITHOUT PARTNERS
P.O. Box 8506
Silver Spring, MD 20907
202-638-1320

CHILD HELP U.S.A.
1345 El Centro Avenue
Hollywood, CA 90028
800-422-4453

AGENCIES SERVING SPECIAL NEEDS CHILDREN

FOUNDATION FOR CHILD DEVELOPMENT
345 East 46th St.
New York, NY 10017
212-697-3150

THE MARCH OF DIMES
1275 Mamaroneck Ave.
White Plains, NY 10605
914-428-7100

INSTITUTE OF PHYSICAL MEDICINE
AND REHABILITATION
New York University Bellevue Medical Center
400 East 34th St.
New York, NY 10016
212-263-6028

AMERICAN MEDICAL ASSOCIATION
Committee on Rehabilitation
535 N. Dearborn St.
Chicago, IL 60610
312-464-5000

AMERICAN DIGESTIVE DISEASE SOCIETY
7720 Wisconsin Avenue
Bethesda, MD 20814

THE UNITED CEREBRAL PALSY ASSOCIATION
66 East 34th Street
New York, NY 10016
212-481-6300

AMERICAN FOUNDATION FOR THE BLIND
15 West 16th Street
New York, NY 10011
212-620-2000

NATIONAL ASSOCIATION
FOR THE VISUALLY HANDICAPPED
22 West 21st Street
New York, NY 10010

THE NATIONAL ASSOCIATION
FOR HEARING AND SPEECH ACTION
10801 Rockville Pike
Rockville, MD 20852
800-638-8255

NATIONAL ASSOCIATION OF THE DEAF
814 Thayer Avenue
Silver Spring, MD 20910
301-587-1788

AMERICAN HEART ASSOCIATION
7320 Greenville Avenue
Dallas, TX 75231
800-527-6941

NATIONAL ASSOCIATION FOR DOWN SYNDROME
628 Ashland
Chicago, IL 60305

NATIONAL EASTER SEAL SOCIETY
2023 West Ogden Avenue
Chicago, IL 60612

Bibliography

Anselmo, Sandra. *Early Childhood Development.* Columbus, Ohio: Merrill Publishing Co. (1987).

Bettelheim, Bruno. *A Good Enough Parent.* New York: Alfred A. Knopf (1987).

Brazelton, T. Berry and Cramer, Bertrand G. *The Earliest Relationship.* Reading, Massachusetts: Addison-Wesley (1990).

Brazelton, T. Berry. *To Listen To A Child.* Reading, Massachusetts: Addison-Wesley (1984).

————. *Infant's and Mother's: Differences in Development.* New York: Delta Books (1983).

————. *On Becoming A Family.* New York: Delacorte Press (1981).

Bredekamp, Sue, ed. *Developmentally Appropriate Practice.* Washington, DC: National Association for the Education of Young Children (1986).

Brody, Robert. "Music Medicine." *Omni* (April 1984).

Brody, Robert and Ingber, Dina. "Music Therapy: Tune-Up for Mind and Body." *Science Digest* (Jan 1982).

Campbell, Don. *Music—Physician for Times to Come* (An Anthology). Wheaton, Ill.: Quest Books (1991).

Canner, Norma. *And A Time To Dance*. Boston, Mass.: Plays, Inc. (1968).

Caplan, Frank ed., *The First Twelve Months of Life*. New York: Perigee (1971).

Debuskey, Mathew, ed., *The Chronically Ill Child and His Family*. Springfield, Illinois: Charles C. Thomas (1970).

Dickinson De Lollis, Rita. "Infant Development Program—Special Care for Special Families." *Children Today* (Jan–Feb. 1985).

Ellis, Havelock. *The Dance of Life*. Westport, Connecticut: Greenwood Press Publishers (1973).

Farran, Christopher. *Infant Colic—What It Is and What You Can Do About It*. New York: Charles Scribner's Sons (1983).

Finlayson, Ann. "The Healing Touch" (treatment of premature babies). *Maclean's* (Dec. 9, 1985).

Fisher, John J. ed., *Johnson and Johnson—From Baby to Toddler.* New York: Putnam (1988).

Freeman, John M., Vining, Eilen P. G., and Pillas, Diana J. *Seizures and Epilepsy in Childhood: A Guide for Parents.* Baltimore, Maryland: The John Hopkins University Press (1990).

Gallagher, Winifred. "Hands-On Infancy" (physical stimulation may have lifelong health effects). *American Health* (Dec 1988).

Gesell, Arnold. *Infant and Child in the Culture of Today.* New York: Harper and Row (1974).

Goode, Erica E. "How Infants See the World." *U.S. News and World Report* (Aug 20, 1990).

Gravelle, Karen. *Understanding Birth Defects.* New York: Frankin Watts (1990).

Healy, Jane M. *Your Child's Growing Mind.* New York: Doubleday (1987).

Hines, William. "Bach for Babies." *Readers Digest* (Oct 1984).

Iyengar, B. K. S. *Light on Yoga.* New York: Schocken Books (1972).

Jason, Janine, and Van Der Meer, Antonia. *Parenting Your Premature Baby.* New York: Henry Holt and Co. (1989).

Jerome, John. *Staying Supple*. New York: Bantam Books (1987).

Kagan, Jerome. *Infancy—Its Place in Human Development*. Cambridge, Massachusetts: Harvard University Press (1978).

Kalweit, Holger. *Dreamtime and Inner Space: The World of the Shaman*. Boston, Massachusetts: Shambhala Publications, Inc. (1988).

Karen, Robert. "Becoming Attached: What Experiences in Infancy Will Enable Children to Thrive Emotionally and to Come to Feel That the World of People is a Positive Place?" *The Atlantic* (Feb 1990).

Kauz, Herman. *Tai Chi Handbook*. New York: Dolphin Books Doubleday and Co., Inc. (1974).

Keasey, Carol Tomlinson. *Child's Eye View*. New York: St. Martin's Press (1980).

Kersey, Katherine. *The Art of Sensitive Parenting*. Washington, D.C.: Acropolis Books (1983).

Koch, Jaroslav. *Total Baby Development*. New York: Wyden Books (1976).

Kunes, Ellen. "The New Fitness Myths." *Working Women Magazine* (1990).

Leach, Penelope. *The First Six Months.* New York: Alfred A. Knopf (1987).

————. *Your Baby and Child From Birth to Age Five.* New York: Alfred A. Knopf (1980).

Lewis, Cynthia Copeland. *Mother's First Year—A Coping Guide for Recent and Prospective Mothers.* Whitehall, Virginia: Betterway Publications (1989).

Lingerman, Hal A. *The Healing Energies of Music.* Wheaton, Illinois: A Quest Book (1983).

Link, David A. ed., *American Baby Guide to Parenting.* New York: Gallery Books (1989).

Maleskey, Gale. "Music That Strikes a Healing Chord: Properly Selected and Used, Music Can Help Dissolve Pain and Stress, and Even Lower Blood Pressure." *Prevention* (Oct 1983).

McAuliffe, Kathleen. "Making of a Mind: The Newborn's Brain." *Omni* (Oct 1985).

McKee, Judy Spitler ed., *Early Childhood Education 88/89.* Connecticut: The Duskin Publishing Group, Inc. (1988–89).

Miezio, Peggy Muller. *Parenting Children With Disabilities.* New York: M. Dekker (1983).

Missett, Judi Sheppard. *The Jazzersize Workout Book*. New York: Charles Scribner's Sons (1986).

Montagu, Ashley. *Touching: The Human Significance of the Skin*. New York: Columbia University Press (1971).

————. *The Human Connection*. New York: McGraw-Hill (1979).

————. *Growing Young*. Massachusetts: Bergin and Garvey (1989).

Ornstein, Robert E. and Sobel, David S. "Getting a Dose of Musical Medicine." *Prevention* (June 1989).

Pirie, Lynne. *Pregnancy and Sports Fitness*. Arizona: Fisher Books (1987).

Pomeranz, Virginia and Shultz, Dodi. "An Infant's Feelings—(Birth to 1 Year)." *Parents' Magazine* (August 1986).

Pueschel, Siegfried M. *A Parent's Guide to Down Syndrome—Toward a Brighter Future*. Baltimore, Maryland: Paul H. Brookes Publishing Co. (1990).

Restak, Richard M. *The Infant Mind*. New York: Doubleday (1986).

Rosas, Debbie, and Rosas, Carlos. *Non-Impact Aerobics—The NIA Technique*. New York: Avon Books (1987).

Roseman, John. *Parent Power! A Common-Sense Approach to Parenting in the 90's and Beyond.* Kansas City, Missouri: Andrews and McMeel (1990).

Rosenfield, Anne H. "Music, the Beautiful Disturber; Whether it's Bach, Beatles, The Boss, Blues or Ballads, Chances are That Music Speaks to Your Emotions, and it's No Accident." *Psychology Today* (Dec 1985).

Rubin, Theodore I. *Child Potential: Fulfilling Your Child's Intellectual, Emotional, and Creative Promise.* New York: Continuum (1990).

Sammons, William A. H. *The Self-Calmed Baby.* Boston: Little Brown (1989).

Samuels, Mike and Nancy. *The Well Baby Book.* New York: Summit Books (1979).

Scofield, Michael and Teich, Mark. "Mind-Bending Music; More and More Mental Health Professionals Are Using Musical Notes to Help People Get Well." *Health* (Feb 1987).

Schuman, Wendy. "Hugs and Kisses; Your Loving Touch Does More Than Comfort Your Children—it is Essential to Their Healthy Development." *Parents' Magazine* (Nov 1984).

Sears, William. *Growing Together: A Parent's Guide to Baby's First Year.* Franklin Park, Illinois: La League International (1987).

Solter, Aletha Jauch. *The Aware Baby: A New Approach to Parenting.* Goleta, California: Shining Star Press (1984).

Stern, Daniel. *The First Relationship's.* Cambridge, Massachusetts: Harvard University Press (1977).

Steinmann, Marion. *The American Medical Association Book of Backcare.* New York: Random House (1982).

Tame, David. *The Secret Power of Music.* New York: Destiny Books (1984).

Time-Life. *Soft Workouts: Low-Impact Exercise.* Alexandria, Virginia: Time-Life Books (1988).

Trotter, Robert J. "The Play's the Thing" (importance of social interaction in infant development). *Psychology Today* (Jan 1987).

Wethered, Audrey. *Movement and Drama in Therapy:* Plays, Inc. (1975).

White, Burton. *A Parent's Guide to the First Three Years.* New Jersey: Prentice-Hall (1980).

Wilson, Frank R. *Tone Deaf and All Thumbs?* New York: Vintage Books (1986).

Wilson, LaVisa Cam. *Infants and Toddlers.* New York: Delmar Publishers, Inc. (1986).